Baseball's Memorable Misses

MISSES

An Unabashed [...] Zeroes

DAN SCHLOSSBERG

Foreword by **DOUGLAS B. LYONS**
Illustrated by **RONNIE JOYNER**

SPORTS PUBLISHING

Copyright © 2023 by Dan Schlossberg
Foreword © 2023 by Douglas B. Lyons
Illustrations © Ronnie Joyner

All rights reserved. No part of this book may be reproduced in
any manner without the express written consent of the publisher,
except in the case of brief excerpts in critical reviews or articles.
All inquiries should be addressed to Sports Publishing, 307 West
36th Street, 11th Floor, New York, NY 10018.

Sports Publishing books may be purchased in bulk at special
discounts for sales promotion, corporate gifts, fund-raising, or
educational purposes. Special editions can also be created to
specifications. For details, contact the Special Sales Department,
Sports Publishing, 307 West 36th Street, 11th Floor, New York,
NY 10018 or sportspubbooks@skyhorsepublishing.com.

Sports Publishing® is a registered trademark of Skyhorse
Publishing, Inc.®, a Delaware corporation.

Visit our website at www.sportspubbooks.com.

10 9 8 7 6 5 4 3 2 1

Library of Congress Cataloging-in-Publication Data is available
on file.

Cover design by David Ter-Avanesyan
Front cover photos courtesy of Getty Images;
   Interior illustrations by Ronnie Joyner
   Interior graphics by Getty Images

ISBN: 978-1-68358-456-8
Ebook ISBN: 978-1-68358-469-8

Printed in China

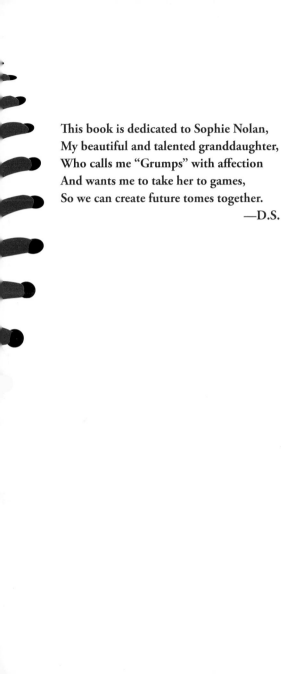

This book is dedicated to Sophie Nolan,
My beautiful and talented granddaughter,
Who calls me "Grumps" with affection
And wants me to take her to games,
So we can create future tomes together.
                                    —D.S.

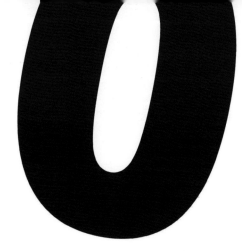

*T*he fact that Dan Schlossberg is a devout fan of the Atlanta Braves while I follow the 27-time world champion New York Yankees does not diminish our friendship. In fact, I think it enhances it.

Neither of us is interested in writing a reverse record book. Here's what I mean: You can look up a record such as MOST WINS IN A CAREER BY A PITCHER: 511 by Cy Young. The reverse record book asks: "Which pitcher won the most games in his career?" Answer: Cy Young. As my father used to say, that's typing, not writing.

Of course, Dan and I are interested in baseball's records. But not so much in the ones that you can simply look up—in the *Baseball Encyclopedia* or more recently online via Wikipedia, *Baseball Almanac*, or Baseball-Reference.com, all invaluable tools for the baseball writer or researcher.

Dan is interested in those achievements and records that you can look up to confirm, but can't look up directly.

For example, in my view, Willie Mays is the greatest player who ever lived. Unlike Babe Ruth and Ty Cobb—both frequently in the conversation about the greatest ballplayer ever—Mays played against the best players of his day, black and white. He is the only outfielder to amass more than 7,000 putouts in a career. Mays also played many games on artificial surface. He played in the era of transcontinental air travel, which often included a day game after a night game in a different time zone. Ruth and Cobb never did. In fact, neither ever played a night game. But despite having amassed 1,909 RBIs, No. 11 on the all-time list, Willie Mays never won a single-season RBI crown.

In 1988, his first year in the National League, Kirk Gibson was selected as Most Valuable Player in the NL with the Los Angeles Dodgers. He was on the winning team in two World Series, won a Silver Slugger award, and was the MVP of the American League Championship Series in 1984 with the Detroit Tigers. But Gibson was never an All-Star. Go figure.

Jim Palmer threw 3,948 innings and gave up 303 home runs over his 19-year Hall of Fame career with the Baltimore Orioles. How can one explain why Palmer never gave up a grand slam?

In this fascinating book, Dan Schlossberg has written many stories about great players and managers—most of them Hall of Famers—who didn't do something: didn't play in a World Series, didn't win a World Series, didn't throw a no-hitter despite a stellar career, didn't win 20 games in a season, didn't win the MVP, didn't hit 50 home runs in a single season, or didn't hit a home run in the same season he won a batting title. All of them earn a big fat Mark of Zero.

Many of these omissions (if they can be called that) are surprising. How could Rod Carew, Rookie of the Year and the 1977 American League MVP, winner of seven American League batting titles, with a career batting average of .328, never have played in a World Series? Likewise, Ernie Banks smashed 512 round-trippers without even a single postseason appearance. Why? Dan has the answers. And thereby hangs a tale. Many tales. Interesting tales indeed.

In my career as a baseball writer, I have been interested in the offbeat and the obscure. [E.g., the only big leaguer whose first and last names include exactly the same letters: Gary Gray. The only man to catch two perfect games: Ron Hassey. An umpire whose license plate reads U R OUT.]

Why? Because others have written the serious analytical books dissecting all the statistics that baseball generates. But just writing, for example, that in a 25-year career Charlie Hough had 216 wins and 216 losses, or that Stan Musial had the same number of hits at home as on the road—1,815 each—doesn't tell the story. It is the stories behind the numbers that fascinate Dan and me.

If you want to read a straightforward book about how great [insert your favorite player's name here] was, or why the [insert the name of your favorite team here] is the greatest team ever, this is not the book for you.

But if you want to read stories about obscure, offbeat achievements and negative accomplishments, Dan has them all right here. Open up and have a few laughs on us.

Enjoy!

Douglas B. Lyons
June 15, 2022

*J*ust as every baseball player is only part of a larger team, every author needs a supporting cast.

When I first suggested *Baseball Zeroes* to Julie Ganz, my talented and terrific editor at Skyhorse, she nodded in enthusiastic agreement. We've worked together before on several projects, including autobiographies of Ron Blomberg and Milo Hamilton and an unorthodox illustrated history of the game called *The New Baseball Bible: Notes, Nuggets, Lists, and Legends from Our National Pastime*.

My teammates on this project also included Doug Lyons, a baseball author and raconteur of considerable note, and the late Ronnie Joyner, by far the best baseball illustrator I've ever seen. Before his untimely demise in March 2022, I enjoyed getting my issues of *Sports Collectors Digest* just so I could see his work.

Thanks also goes to Cooperstown colleagues Jim Gates, Jeff Idelson, Cassidy Lent, Bruce Markusen, Craig Muder, Josh Rawitch, and Tim Mead, all current or former employees of the Baseball Hall of Fame. I love that place—and love talking about my books during their Author Series in the Bullpen Theater.

Even before my first talk there, I became a member of the Society for American Baseball Research, an organization of fans, writers, researchers, and historians whose collective love and knowledge of the game has no equal.

The list of SABR friends is long and lengthy but topped by Marc Appelman, Evelyn Begley, Maxwell Kates, Howie Siegel, John Vorperian, and that Lyons guy again.

Longtime friend and colleague John Thorn, official historian of Major League Baseball, is a fountain of knowledge too. So is Jayson Stark, a fellow Syracuse grad who shares my love of oddities and ironies—many of them mentioned in the pages that follow.

For sheer longevity of friendship, Marty Appel, Kevin Barnes, Barry Bloom, Bill Jacobowitz, and Bob Ibach have been cherished friends for decades. I've known Dave Cohen a long time too—dating back to my Syracuse University days—while fellow Atlanta resident Chuck Simon is a relative newcomer but definitely a keeper. That proves that baseball love transcends political differences.

Thanks also to Steve Borelli of *USA TODAY Sports Weekly*, Rick Cerrone of *Baseball Digest*, Brett Knight and Matthew Craig of forbes.com, Julio Pabon and Nicole Perez of Latino Sports, and my terrific literary agent, Rob Wilson, who had the misfortune to be a minor-league first baseman in the Yankees system behind somebody named Don Mattingly.

Hugs to Linda Rosen, who became a friend and fellow author after starting as my aerobics instructor, and to Nancy Whittaker, whose Latino Cardio class at the Fair Lawn Senior Center fills up so fast that it pays to get there early just to reserve a spot. I have yet to figure out how Linda and Nancy can be so upbeat so early; as a part-time curmudgeon, I'm a morning grouch.

Thanks also to Barry and Katonya Rochester, the husband-and-wife fitness tandem who met in a dance contest and filled in admirably—even on Zoom—when COVID interfered with all our lives. And thanks to the doctors, nurses, and pharmacists who gave me shots, boosters, and encouragement when all odds indicated things would be different.

For friends who may have missed my company and my jokes while I was working on this book, I am also deeply indebted.

So, thank you Larry Cancro, Al Clark, Ilene Dorf Manahan, David Fenster, Allen Gross, Muggsy Hamilton (Milo's son), Jay Horwitz, Larry Horwitz, Jason Hyman, Maggie Linton, Jim Lovell, Bill Menzel, Brian Mullen, Bob Muscatell, Maryellen Nugent Lee, Bonnie and Ken Olivenbaum, Phyllis and Bruce Palley, Sam and Linda Rosen, and the late Ed Lucas, Mitch Packer, and Ira Silverman, whom I miss every day.

And last but certainly not least, I could not have completed this project without the support and understanding of Phyllis Deutsch, Ali Nolan, Sophie Nolan, Jenny O'Rourke, and Samantha Schlossberg.

*E*very day of the long baseball season, from mid-February right into November, something happens that never happened before.

That happens during the offseason too.

Then there's a long list of things that *never* happened and never will.

Baseball Zeroes—the end result—was a twinkle in my mind's eye for years before I decided it would make a terrific tongue-in-cheek book.

When I was an adjunct professor for Institute in Learning Retirement (ILR) at Bergen Community College, my course was called "Baseball Oddities & Ironies."

This book is full of them—and expanding every day.

Zero Mostel never threw out the first ball at a game, as my fellow author and foreword writer had hoped, but Don Mattingly did have zero grand slams in his career—except for the single season when he hit six, more than any previous player.

Stan Musial hit five home runs in a day and 475 in his career but won zero home run titles.

Even Willie Mays earned a zero: he had that many RBI crowns.

And how about Nolan Ryan, who played the longest, struck out the most hitters, and threw the most no-hitters? He had exactly zero Cy Young Awards.

At the opposite extreme, Roger Clemens, Greg Maddux, and Steve Carlton combined for 15 Cy Youngs but—you guessed it—zero no-hitters! And let's not forget that Clemens also was the only man to craft two nine-inning, 20-strikeout games—amazingly, 10 years apart.

Even managers are included in the pages that follow. Bobby Cox, ejected a record 158 times during the regular season and three more in postseason play, got a zero in his column because he earned that many ejections from longtime umpire Al Clark, another old-school guy.

All the greats of the game are here:

- Zero games in which Hank Aaron hit for the cycle
- Zero times Aaron won a Triple Crown
- Zero times National League teams traded managers
- Zero Sunday games for Branch Rickey

There are even cases of double zeroes—a uniform number worn by Paul Dade—and triple zeroes—the team batting average of the Chicago White Sox before and after Bob Feller no-hit them on Opening Day.

And pity the poor Baltimore Orioles of 1988. They had zero wins in their first 21 games, a record virtually certain to stand the test of time.

National League Most Valuable Players from the New York Mets? Zero.

All-Star Game appearances by Kirk Gibson? Nada—not even in the year he was NL MVP.

World Series games for Ernie Banks? Not one.

Grand slams by Pete Alonso when he hit a rookie record 53 homers? Bupkis.

Games Jack Norworth saw before writing *Take Me Out to the Ballgame*? Zero!

And let's not forget Albert Pujols making his first appearance as a pitcher at age 42 after playing 2,987 games and hitting 681 home runs. That means zero games pitched for the three-time MVP before 2022.

Not to mention zero home runs for another 42-year-old—Bartolo Colon—before connecting for his first at Petco Park. *Nobody* else was that old when hitting his first.

Baseball Zeroes is a virtual gold mine that will thrill trivia buffs and convince even rabid fans that they didn't know it all after all.

Like a chef hoping his patrons rave about his cooking, I hope readers revel in this concept. The best thing they can say? "Gee, I didn't know that!"

Leave it on the coffee table or the top of the toilet. This book is meant to be opened to any page and even read backwards.

It's perfect for rain delays, long commercials between innings, or dreary winters that never seem to end.

I hope it will convince anyone who believes baseball is no longer the national pastime to change his or her mind quickly.

I also hope reading it will be as much fun as writing it. *Bon chance!*

Dan Schlossberg
Fair Lawn, NJ
June 15, 2022

Teams

0 Defeats suffered by the 1869 Cincinnati Red Stockings, the first professional team. They played 69 games and one game ended in a tie.

0 Home runs in 1906 World Series. Neither the White Sox nor Cubs connected over the course of that six-game, all-Chicago World Series during the Deadball Era.

0 At-bats in the majors for Archibald Wright Graham. While a med student at Maryland University, he began to "moonlight" as a minor-league player. Called up by the New York Giants in 1905, he got into a game as an outfield replacement but never batted. Though he won a minor-league batting title, he also graduated from med school and became a full-time doctor in 1909. His baseball nickname survived, however, thanks to the film *Field of Dreams*.

Image Credit: Ronnie Joyner

0 AL teams that wore pinstripes before 1912. That was the year the Yankees, then known as Highlanders, became the first.

0 World Series sweeps before 1914. Boston's "Miracle" Braves, dead last on July 19, staged a stunning finish that lasted through the Fall Classic against Connie Mack's Philadelphia Athletics. The A's, favored to sweep, failed to win even a single game from the Braves, who won their only world championship that year as denizens of Boston.

0 Teams with turtle emblems. Only the Baltimore Terrapins, a Federal League team that lasted two years, had a terrapin image on their uniforms because the freshwater turtle was found in the nearby Chesapeake Bay.

Image Credit: Ronnie Joyner

0 Players nicknamed by a collision—except for Crash Davis. Lawrence Columbus Davis got his nickname playing high school ball in Georgia. Playing shortstop, he crashed into the left fielder, who was chasing the same pop fly. He spent three years with the Philadelphia Athletics but a lifetime with the nickname, later popularized by the Kevin Costner film *Bull Durham*.

0 Deadball teams with numbers. The Cleveland Indians wore numbers on their sleeves as a one-year experiment in 1916 and the New York Yankees became the first to wear permanent numbers in 1929. The Yankee numerals matched player slots in the lineup. Rules requiring numbers were not enacted until 1937.

0 Numbers worn by Ty Cobb and Christy Mathewson. Both played before numbers became universal.

00 Uniform number worn by Cardinals pitcher Omar Olivares reflective of his initials. Why Paul Dade also wore it we don't know, but it might have been well-deserved self-deprecation (he was a utilityman who always seemed to be the 25th man on his team's roster).

Image Credit: Ronnie Joyner

0 American League players with 22 total bases in one day. Thanks to a doubleheader, Al Oliver of the Texas Rangers compiled 21, an AL record, on August 17, 1980. He hit .303 lifetime.

09 Uniform number worn by San Diego Padres Benito Santiago, who said catchers shouldn't wear a single digit because that number would be hidden behind the back strap of their chest protector.

0 Number worn by Oddibe McDowell, Al Oliver, Rey Ordoñez, Junior Ortiz, Adam Ottavino, Mallex Smith, Marcus Stroman, and a dozen others who would otherwise be forgotten if not for this book.

0 Dollars gamblers gave Buck Weaver to fix the World Series. The star third baseman of the Chicago White Sox was asked to join the conspiracy but refused, then played well during the 1919

Image Credit: Ronnie Joyner

0 Known locations of plaque to Ray Chapman. Installed at Cleveland's League Park after the shortstop suffered a fatal beaning in 1920, the plaque eventually moved to Municipal Stadium and Progressive Field. But it was missing for several years before turning up again.

Fall Classic. Weaver led both the Sox and the Reds with five extra-base hits while batting .324, hardly stats that suggest he was throwing games. Yet he was one of the eight Black Sox banned by Commissioner Kenesaw Mountain Landis in 1920. "Regardless of the verdict of juries," Landis said, "no player who throws a game, no player that sits in a conference with a bunch of crooked players and gamblers where the ways and means of throwing games are planned and discussed and does not promptly tell his club about it will ever play professional baseball." The eight men banned, including Weaver, had their records expunged and were prohibited from even buying tickets to future games.

0 Tripleheaders after 1920. One was played between the Pittsburgh Pirates and Cincinnati Reds on October 2 of that year, none since.

0 Players paid $100,000 on the 1927 Yankees. Babe Ruth's $70,000 salary topped the payroll.

0 Teams with regular numbers before 1929. Although the Cleveland Indians tried wearing uniform numbers as early as 1916, the first team to don them on a regular basis was the 1929 New York Yankees. Numbers were handed out according to each player's position in the lineup.

0 National League teams that went 300 games without being shut out. The New York Yankees, an American League team, had a 308-game streak in the '30s.

0 Team hats before 1930 with a single sock logo. The 1931 Boston Red Sox hat was the only one that had just a single sock.

2 Big-league lefties named Luis Tiant. Known for his twisting windup and Fu Manchu mustache, Luis Tiant was a four-time 20-game winner who won 122 games for the Boston Red Sox and helped pitch the team to the 1975 AL pennant. He threw right-handed though his father, pitching in Cuba and the Negro Leagues, threw from the port side.

Image Credit: Ronnie Joyner

0 Rules requiring teams to wear uniform numbers before 1937. As noted earlier, the Indians experimented with numbers on sleeves in 1916 and the Yankees began using them on a regular basis in 1929, but the leagues did not make numbers mandatory for another eight years.

.000 Team batting average of 1940 Chicago White Sox before and after Opening Day. They were victims of a Bob Feller no-hitter—the first one ever pitched in the first game of the season.

0 Teams that lost 20 doubleheaders in a season. The 1943 Philadelphia Athletics hold the record with 18 in a year that also included 20 straight losses and 105 overall.

0 Runs scored by New York Giants in three-way game. Although the Giants hosted a wartime fundraiser at the Polo Grounds on

Image Credit: Ronnie Joyner

0 Appearances by Carl Erskine in the Bobby Thomson game. Normally a starter, Erskine was a prospective ninth-inning reliever before he bounced a curve while warming up in the bullpen—convincing Dodgers manager Charlie Dressen to summon Ralph Branca instead. Thomson's three-run homer gave the Giants a 5-4 victory and the NL pennant.

June 26, 1944, they failed to score. The Brooklyn Dodgers won the six-inning exhibition game, scoring five runs, while the New York Yankees managed just one. More than 50,000 fans watched the game, which allowed each team to play successive innings against the other two and then sit out an inning.

0 Balls hit over the fence by the 1945 Washington Senators at their own ballpark. The team hit 27 homers but only one—an inside-the-park shot by Joe Kuhel—at Griffith Stadium, their home park.

0 Major league teams with .300 batting averages since 1950. The Boston Red Sox, who hit .302 that year, were the last ball-club to produce such a solid team average in a single season.

0 Opening Day night games before 1950. The Cards beat the Pirates, 4–2, in that April 17 game at Sportsman's Park, St. Louis. Many teams now start their seasons at night.

0 Days alone in first place for the 1951 New York Giants before the last day of the season. The Giants won, taking sole possession of first place, and had to await the outcome of the Dodgers game. Brooklyn beat Philadelphia, 9-8, in 10 innings to knot the race again and force a best-of-three playoff settled by Bobby Thomson's "shot heard 'round the world" in the ninth inning of the decisive Game 3 at the Polo Grounds. Thomson's two-run homer was also the difference in the first game, a 3–1 victory for the Giants at Brooklyn's Ebbets Field. The Dodgers won the second game, 10–0, behind rookie Clem Labine. The Giants finished with a 98–59 record, one game better than Brooklyn's 97–60 record.

0 Teams that topped 15 runs in the first inning. The Brooklyn Dodgers own the major-league mark. Helped by a Duke Snider homer, they scored a record 15 times against Cincinnati on May 21, 1952, at Ebbets Field.

Image Credit: Ronnie Joyner

0 Number of intentional walks Roger Maris received during his 61-homer season. Mickey Mantle was batting behind him.

0 Prewar MVPs from losing teams. That trend ended in 1952, when voters from the Baseball Writers Association of America named Hank Sauer of the Chicago Cubs their choice in the National League.

0 Teams with 10-game losing streaks that became world champions. The 1953 New York Yankees, with nine straight, had the longest losing streak by a team that won the World Series that same season.

0 Prewar teams that scored a dozen runs in an inning before making an out. The Brooklyn Dodgers did it in 1953 and the Boston Red Sox matched the feat in 2009.

Image Credit: Ronnie Joyner

0 American League third basemen not named Brooks Robinson who won Gold Gloves while Brooks was playing the position for Baltimore from 1960 to 1975. He spent his entire 23-year career with the Orioles.

0 World championships for the Dodgers before 1955. That was the year Brooklyn won its only World Series, helped in part by a great outfield catch by Sandy Amoros against Yogi Berra.

0 Red Sox rosters with black players before 1959. That was the year Boston became the final team to integrate, adding infielder Pumpsie Green. He tripled off the Green Monster in his first at-bat.

0 Wins for the 1961 Phillies between games started by John Buzhardt. The team lost a record 23 in a row but won games started by the otherwise forgettable Buzhardt on both ends of the dubious streak. Just for the record, Buzhardt wore uniform No. 23.

0 Houston major-league teams before 1962. The Houston Colt .45s, a National League expansion franchise, began play in 1962

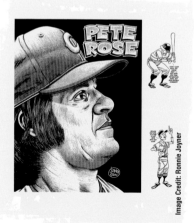

0 Number of hits Pete Rose got in his first 11 at-bats. A 17-time All-Star who was National League Rookie of the Year and eventual Most Valuable Player, the versatile Rose got off to a slow start but finished with a record 4,256 hits before becoming a full-time manager.

Image Credit: Ronnie Joyner

in an open-air ballpark but summer heat forced the team to stage the first Sunday night games and eventually to build a domed ballpark, the Houston Astrodome.

0 Wins in first nine games for original Mets. The expansion New York Mets of 1962 lost their first nine games en route to a 60–120 record. Mets starters combined for 23 wins—fewer than Don Drysdale (25) or Jack Sanford (24) and as many as Ralph Terry and Bob Purkey.

0 Games outside US borders before 1969. That was the first year the expansion Montreal Expos brought America's national pastime to Canada.

Image Credit: Ronnie Joyner

0 Runs allowed by Orel Hershiser during record scoreless innings streak. The star right-hander of the Los Angeles Dodgers worked a record 59 consecutive scoreless innings in 1988. Later that year, he was selected Most Valuable Player of both the NL Championship Series and World Series and winner of a World Series ring and both the NL's Cy Young and Gold Glove awards. Hershiser was later MVP in an American League Championship Series.

0 Winning seasons by the Seattle Pilots. The hapless 1969 expansion team lasted one year before becoming the Milwaukee Brewers.

0 Opening Day wins for the Mets before their "miracle." The National League expansion team lost eight straight openers before their surprise world championship season of 1969.

0 American League teams named for World's Fairs. Only the National League's Montreal Expos, a team that lasted from 1969 through 2004 before becoming the Washington Nationals, were named after the exposition.

0 Winning seasons by second-edition Senators when not managed by Ted Williams. The expansion team enjoyed its only plus-.500 season when the Hall of Fame slugger served as its manager from 1969 to 1971.

0 Losses in first two weeks by the 1982 Atlanta Braves, who opened the season with a 13-game winning streak en route to a playoff spot that fall. Their record was later tied by the Milwaukee Brewers.

0 Teams before 1987 that started a game with three straight homers. Then the San Diego Padres did it on April 13, getting consecutive homers in their home opener from Marvell Wynne, Tony Gwynn, and John Kruk.

0 Wins in first 21 games for 1988 Orioles. The 0–21 Birds finally broke through but brought home a 1–23 mark on May 2, promoted as "Fantastic Fans" night by the team. In front of 52,000 fans at Memorial Stadium, the team announced it would

build a new baseball-only ballpark in the old Baltimore & Ohio Railroad yards. The final details were written on the back of a menu in an Amtrak club car earlier that day.

O Double worst-to-first teams until 1991. That was the first year two teams jumped from last the year before to first-place finishes in divisional races. The Minnesota Twins jumped from a 74–88 season to a 95–67 mark and surprise world championship, while the Atlanta Braves improved by 29 games, finishing with 94 wins. That started a string of 14 straight division crowns, a record no team has come close to challenging.

O Multiple worst-to-first teams between 1991 and 2007. The Chicago Cubs, under new manager Lou Piniella, went from last in 2006 to first in 2007 with a 90-win season. At the same time, the Arizona Diamondbacks won 32 one-run games to finish with a matching 90–72 mark, giving them a half-game margin over the Colorado Rockies in the NL West. Four years later, Arizona would become the first team to jump from worst to first three times.

O Victories for the Rockies against the Braves in 1993. The NL expansion club went 0–13 against Atlanta, allowing the Braves to win 104 games, one more than San Francisco, to take the NL West title (the Braves moved to the East in 1994).

O Wild-card teams until 1994. When the San Francisco Giants won 103 games but finished one game behind the Atlanta Braves in the 1993 National League West race, baseball officials created three-division play that included a wild-card—the second-place team with the best record. Additional wild-card winners were added to the playoff system years later.

◊ Replacement players for the Baltimore Orioles. Although most major-league teams hired replacements for striking players in the spring of 1995, the Orioles would not. Owner Peter Angelos, a labor lawyer, cancelled his schedule of exhibition games on March 20 and the Maryland House of Delegates barred replacement players for all teams scheduled to play in Camden Yards. The Toronto Blue Jays also did not use replacements.

◊ NL teams with worse starts than the 1997 Cubs. They lost their first 12, two more than the previous worst record by the 1988 Braves and one more than the 1884 Detroit Wolverines.

◊ First-place finishes for Miami Marlins. The Florida Marlins, the team's original name, never finished first either—but twice won world championships after entering the playoffs as a wild-card team. They were the first wild-card team to win the World Series but not the only one.

◊ Winning seasons for Tampa Bay Devil Rays. The minute the 1977 expansion team dropped the word *devil* from their nickname, they enjoyed their first winning season. They even posted the best record in the American League that year, 2008. After finishing last nine times in its first ten seasons, Tampa Bay suddenly caught fire under innovative manager Joe Maddon and won its first divisional crown. Powered by a pitching staff that placed second in earned run average, the Rays reached the World Series but lost to Philadelphia.

◊ Teams that won 15 straight World Series games. The Yankees had 14 before the Mets ended the streak during the Subway Series of 2000.

Ⓞ Teams eliminated by contraction. After MLB voted to eliminate Minnesota and Montreal in 2001, the Twins sued, thus saving their franchise. Contraction never happened, though Montreal later relocated to Washington.

Ⓞ World Series wins by Atlanta Braves at Turner Field. When the Braves went all the way in 1995 and 2021, their home fields were Atlanta Fulton County Stadium and Truist Park, respectively.

Ⓞ Israeli flags on twentieth-century major-league uniforms. The blue-and-white national emblem of Israel appeared on the sleeves of Houston Astros uniforms in 2003 after Israeli astronaut Ilan Ramon was killed in the reentry explosion of the space

Image Credit: Ronnie Joyner

Ⓞ Days Nate Colbert spent nursing his injured knee in 1972. The slugging San Diego first baseman hurt his knee in a home-plate collision on July 31 in Atlanta but decided he didn't want to miss any games at Atlanta Fulton County Stadium, a ballpark known as "the Launching Pad" because it was so hitter-friendly. Colbert made the right decision, as he hit five home runs and knocked in 13 runs during a doubleheader the next day.

shuttle Columbia. He had trained at the Johnson Space Center in Houston.

◯ Rookies of the Year from the Pittsburgh Pirates during the twentieth century. Even though the award was inaugurated in 1947, the first top rookie in Pirates livery was Jason Bay in 2004.

◯ Teams with four straight 100-win seasons. Five teams, most recently the 2004 Yankees, have done it three years in a row.

◯ "I's" in the McDonald's Big Mac sign after homer. Cardinals slugger Albert Pujols hit a first-inning home run on May 21, 2009, that knocked the "I" out of the word "Big" in the left-field advertising sign at Busch Stadium.

◯ Pennants for Texas Rangers before 2010. Created in 1972 by the transfer of the second-edition Washington Senators to the Dallas-Fort Worth metro area, the team did not reach the World Series until 2010.

◯ Teams that played in five different divisions. The Milwaukee Brewers hold the record with four: East (1972–93), Central (1994–97), and West (1969–71) in the American League and Central (1998-present) in the National.

◯ Teams with three slams in a game before 2011. The Yankees did it on August 25, 2011, when Robinson Cano, Curtis Granderson, and Russell Martin connected.

◯ Teams with eight 20-homer men before 2014. The Minnesota Twins did it in 2019 en route to a team-record 307 homers.

O AL teams to start game with three straight homers in the twentieth century. The Baltimore Orioles became the first on May 10, 2012. Ryan Flaherty, J. J. Hardy, and Nick Markakis were the sluggers who did it.

O Teams that won more than 10 straight postseason elimination games. The San Francisco Giants won 10 straight from 2012 to 2016 en route to three world championships.

O Pirates playoff spots for 20 years starting in 1993. Pittsburgh finally reached the postseason in 2013, but its success was short-lived.

O Teams with six playoff shutouts. Cleveland had a record five in 2016 but lost the World Series—even though they blanked the Chicago Cubs twice.

O Road wins in World Series by the 2017 Astros. The team won all four games at Minute Maid Park, helped in part by an elaborate sign-stealing system that cost the jobs of manager A. J. Hinch and general manager Jeff Luhnow when discovered by Major League Baseball.

O Players with five teams in a season before 2018. Then the illustrious Oliver Drake became the first one to do that.

O Seasons that three teams had 100-win seasons before 2018. That year, the Red Sox, Yankees, and Astros did it. One year later, the Yankees and Astros did it again, along with the Twins.

0 Cleveland losses during a 22-game streak in 2017. The Indians won 22 straight, an American League record, that season.

0 Paid attendance for Oakland A's anniversary game. On April 17, 2018, the Athletics admitted all fans free to mark their 50th anniversary in the Bay Area.

0 Home wins in World Series by 2019 Astros. No team had lost all its home games before. The winning Nationals brought Washington its first world championship in 95 years.

0 Players with one team longer than Brooks Robinson. The Baltimore third baseman spent all 23 years with the Orioles, sharing the mark for one-team longevity with Boston's Carl Yastrzemski.

0 National League teams wearing Braille jerseys. The Baltimore Orioles, an American League club, were the first to do that, on September 26, 2018. They also wore green jerseys and caps for Earth Day, April 22, earlier that year.

0 National League teams that hit six home runs before making six outs. The Houston Astros of the American League were the first in 2019.

0 Twentieth-century teams with four road wins in World Series. The 2019 Washington Nationals became the first to do that, defeating the favored Houston Astros.

0 Chief Wahoo logos on Cleveland uniforms. The racist logo left before the 2019 season, three years before the Indians nickname also disappeared in favor of Guardians.

0   Teams with four straight 100-win seasons. The Houston Astros might have done that if the 2020 season had not been shortened to 60 games by the COVID-19 pandemic.

0   National League teams of the Modern Era with 30 runs in a game. The Atlanta Braves plated 29, an NL mark, against the Miami Marlins during the virus-shortened 2020 season.

0   Teams with 20 pinch homers in a season. The 2021 San Francisco Giants had a record 18.

0   Number of division titles for Miami Marlins. A 1993 NL expansion team originally named the Florida Marlins, this club was the first wild-card team to win a world championship. In 1997, the Fish beat Cleveland on a walk-off single in the 11th inning of Game 7. Six years later, another wild-card Marlins team beat the Yankees in the World Series, giving the Florida franchise two world titles but no division crowns.

0   Washington Nationals retired numbers before 2022. On June 18, the team honored retired first baseman Ryan Zimmerman by retiring his No. 11. The Nationals had inherited several retired numbers from their original incarnation as the Montreal Expos but had never retired a number for a Nationals original before Zimmerman. The Montreal honorees were Andre Dawson, Gary Carter, Tim Raines, and Rusty Staub.

0   Twentieth-century teams that used mannequins to show players the "uniform of the day." A clubhouse store mannequin nicknamed Manny found its way into the Washington Nationals clubhouse early in the 2019 season. With 18 potential uniform

combinations, the players knew what uniform to wear when they saw how Manny was dressed. The idea must have worked: the Nats won their only world championship that very season.

◯ Players whose numbers were retired four times. The record is three, shared by Frank Robinson and Nolan Ryan. And only Robinson's No. 20 was retired three times; Ryan wore No. 30 for the Angels but No. 34 for the Astros and Rangers.

◯ Mets who wore No. 8 after Gary Carter. Though the uniform is not officially retired, the team has not reissued it since Carter left.

◯ Teams that lost three no-hitters in one season before 2021. That's when the Cleveland Indians became the first.

◯ Teams that went worst-to-first four times. The Arizona Diamondbacks did it three times, more than any other club.

◯ American League worst-to-first teams before the Red Sox did it twice. The Boston Red Sox went from last place one year to first place the next—in two different seasons.

◯ Three-way, end-of-season ties. Close calls many times, though.

◯ Twentieth-century world champions who were under .500 in August. The 2021 Atlanta Braves entered August under .500, finally climbing above that mark on August 6, en route to a surprise world championship. The Braves won 44 games over the second half but wound up with just 88 wins, fewest of any playoff participant, before they went 11–6 in postseason play, winning each of three series without stretching any of them to the max.

Atlanta won the best-of-five Division Series against Milwaukee in four games, the best-of-seven Championship Series against Los Angeles in six, and the best-of-seven World Series against Houston in six.

0 Teams no-hit more than 20 times. The Philadelphia Phillies were victimized for a record 20th time in 2022 when five New York Mets pitchers held them hitless in April.

0 Regular-season games played by Dodgers at old Yankee Stadium. Although they played many post-season games at the original Yankee Stadium, in use from 1923–2008, the Dodgers were the only team that never played a regular-season game there. Although interleague play began in 1977, the Los Angeles Dodgers were never scheduled for a series in the Bronx.

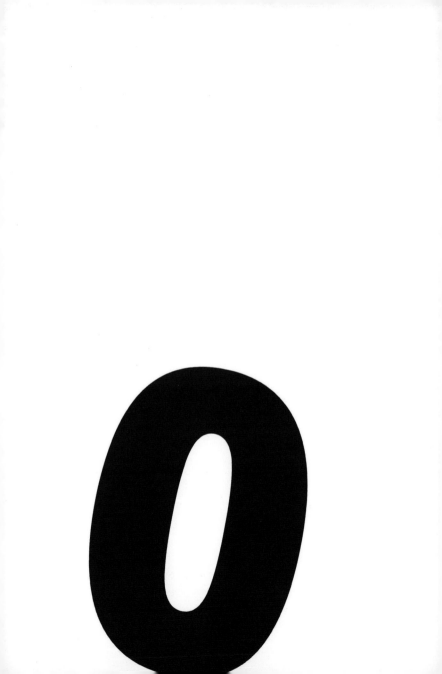

Hitters

0 Modern Era pitchers who won batting titles. But it happened in 1886, when Guy Hecker of Louisville won 27 games as a pitcher, played first base or the outfield when not on the mound, and led the American Association—then a major league—with a .342 batting average. Baseball's Modern Era began in 1901 with the advent of the American League and the beginning of the two-league format that has been in force ever since.

0 Inside-the-park home runs by anyone with a four-homer game in the Modern Era. The only four-homer hitter who went inside-the-park was Ed Delahanty in 1896—and he did twice.

0 American League teams with 30 hits in a game. The major-league record is 31 by the New York Giants on June 9, 1901. They victimized the Cincinnati Reds, 25–13.

0 Hitters with 30 home runs prior to the Roaring Twenties. Babe Ruth hit 29, then the record, in 1919 before breaking out with 59 in 1920, his first full year with the Yankees and his first as a position player.

0 Fatalities on the field after Ray Chapman. Beaned by a Carl Mays pitch in 1920, the Cleveland shortstop was the only major-leaguer killed on the field. But it took nearly 40 years before helmets became universal.

0 Number of ways Joe Jackson tried to fix the 1919 World Series. Though one of the eight men banned from the game by Commissioner Kenesaw Mountain Landis, Jackson led both teams with a .375 batting average, hit the only home run of the controversial Fall Classic between the White Sox and Reds, and did not make any errors in the field. His left-handed swing was copied by Babe Ruth.

Image Credit: Ronnie Joyner

0 Games as Yankees captain for Babe Ruth in 1922. American League president Ban Johnson fined the controversial slugger, suspended him for five days, and prevented him from continuing as Yankees captain.

0 Sports Babe Ruth couldn't play. He actually won more awards for golf than he did for baseball.

0 Over-the-fence home runs by Tommy Thevenow. In 15 years and 4,164 at-bats, the 5–10, 155-pound infielder never hit the ball over the fence. He did have an inside-the-park home run for the Cardinals in the 1926 World Series, however, and two during the regular season that year.

0 Suspensions given to Ty Cobb and Tris Speaker for alleged game fixing. Both were investigated but not punished.

0 Seasons Rogers Hornsby was 200 batting runs, 50 fielding runs, and 25 league-winning runs above average among second basemen. The only second basemen to do that were Jackie Robinson and Lou Whitaker.

0 Double-play tandems with 500 games played. Detroit's Lou Whitaker and Alan Trammell had a record 4,459.

0 Pitchers unable to prevent RBI record. Hack Wilson of the Chicago Cubs collected 191 RBIs in 1930 because his table-setters Kiki Cuyler and Woody English had on-base percentages of .428 and .430, respectively.

0 Major leaguers with three homers in an inning. It's happened only once in professional baseball—when Gene Rye was in the Texas League on August 6, 1930. En route to a 22–4 win over Beaumont, Rye's Waco team enjoyed an 18-run inning. He led off with a home run and subsequently delivered two more, giving him 12 total bases, nine extra bases, and eight RBIs—records that remain intact.

0 National Leaguers who led the league in home runs and stolen bases since Chuck Klein. The Phillies slugger was the last man to turn the unique double, in 1932.

Almost **0**. Joe Sewell's strikeout total in 1932. He fanned three times in 576 plate appearances.

0 Bats broken by Joe Sewell. En route to 2,226 hits, the ultimate contact hitter kept his favorite bat, "Black Betty," rubbed with chewing tobacco and rolled it with a Coke bottle.

0 Catchers other than Mickey Cochrane to hit for the cycle twice. The dynamic Detroit backstop delivered in successive seasons, 1932–33.

0 Sixty-homer seasons for Jimmie Foxx. Variously called The Beast or Double-X, Foxx was a feared slugger stymied in his bid to break Babe Ruth's 1927 record by ballpark changes designed to prevent "cheap" home runs. As a result, in 1932, Foxx hit five balls off the new screen at Sportsman's Park in St. Louis and three off a similar barrier erected in left field at Cleveland's League Park. All eight would have been homers in previous years and cost Foxx, who wound up with 58, the chance to beat the Babe.

0 Four-homer games by Jimmie Foxx. In 1933 he hit four consecutive home runs over two games in June. It was the first time in the Modern Era anyone hit four in a row.

0 Fielding chances for Lou Gehrig at shortstop. Plagued by back trouble, the durable Yankees slugger nearly missed a game in 1934. Rather than interrupt his consecutive games playing streak, however, manager Joe McCarthy turned in a lineup listing Gehrig as leadoff man and shortstop—even though he threw left-handed. Gehrig singled in the top of the first but never took the field. He did, however, preserve his streak and go on go win his only Triple Crown that year.

0 Personal distractions affecting Lou Gehrig's streak. The durable first baseman, dubbed The Iron Man, even played on the day he was married—continuing a consecutive games playing streak that stretched to 2,130 games.

0 Openers for Lou Gehrig after 1939. He started for the Yankees, had no hits, and made an error. On July 4 of that year, he told Yankee Stadium fans he was "the luckiest man on the face of the earth." He died two years later of ALS.

0 Players before World War II with two pinch homers on the same day. Joe Cronin became the first on June 17, 1943.

0 Wartime major-league action for Hank Greenberg. The Detroit slugger spent four years in the military during World War II but came back in time to hit a ninth-inning grand slam against the St. Louis Browns that clinched the 1945 pennant. Had the Tigers lost both ends of that doubleheader, they would have had a one-game pennant playoff with Washington.

Image Credit: Ronnie Joyner

0 National League Triple Crown winners after Joe Medwick. The Cardinals outfielder led the league in batting, home runs, and runs batted in during the 1937 season. Nobody in the NL has done it since.

0 Senators balls that cleared the Griffith Stadium fences in 1945. The wartime Washington Senators had only 27 home runs—and just one (an inside-the-parker by Joe Kuhel) in the cavernous Washington ballpark. The stadium measured 405 to left, 421 to center, and 320 to right. In 19 seasons, Hall of Famer Sam Rice never hit the ball over the fence there.

0 American Leaguers with six runs scored in a game before World War II. Boston shortstop Johnny Pesky became the first on May 8, 1946, during a 14–10 Red Sox win over the White Sox. He went 4-for-5 with a walk and two runs batted in while matching Mel Ott's major-league mark.

0 Inside-the-park home runs by Ted Williams after 1946. The one he hit that year, the only one of his 521 that did not clear an outfield fence, clinched the pennant for the Red Sox in Cleveland.

0 American Leaguers with more home runs than strikeouts during 50-homer seasons. Only Johnny Mize, who played in the National League with the New York Giants, did that, when he had 51 homers and 42 strikeouts in 1947.

0 Major-league games for Josh Gibson. Widely considered the Babe Ruth of the Negro Leagues, he never got a chance to play in the established big leagues before he died of a brain tumor in 1947. Years later, on December 16, 2020, Major League Baseball announced that the Negro Leagues would be re-classified as major leagues–but Gibson never knew it at the time.

0 Players with a .500 career on-base percentage. Ted Williams actually came close with .482, the major-league record.

0 MVP trophies for Ted Williams in Triple Crown seasons. Wildly unpopular with voting writers, he lost MVP votes to Joe Gordon in 1942 and Joe DiMaggio in 1949.

0 NL players who led in all Triple Crown categories more than twice. The only man to do that was Ted Williams, who led the American League in hitting and home runs six times each and runs batted in four times. National Leaguer Rogers Hornsby came close, with seven batting crowns, two home run titles, and four most-RBI campaigns.

0 Triple Crown winners who also led their leagues in stolen bases.

0 Years the DiMaggio brothers played together. Vince, Dom, and Joe were never teammates.

0 Songs about Vince DiMaggio. One of three DiMaggio brothers to become big-league outfielders, he was never good enough to have a song written about him—as brother Joe did—but made his own music singing opera with his strong voice.

0 Years in which Dom DiMaggio led his league in errors. In fact, he's the only one of the three DiMaggio brothers to avoid that dubious distinction. Dom, the youngest, also led his league in assists three times, as opposed to twice for Vince and once for Joe.

0 Players with a dozen World Series rings. Yogi Berra won a record 10 and also played in the most World Series games (75) and collected the most hits (71).

0 American League players with four MVP awards. Yogi Berra and several others share the AL record with three, while National Leaguer Barry Bonds won seven.

0 Catchers before Yogi Berra who kept a finger outside the mitt. The three-time American League MVP did it to reduce the beating on the left (glove) hand by putting more padding between hand and ball. Many followed his lead.

0 Catchers who caught 3,000 games. Hall of Famer Pudge Rodriguez was behind the plate a record 2,427 times.

0 Seasons with 400 total bases by Willie, Mickey, or the Duke. The short list of players who produced seasons with 400 total bases does not include a single season by Willie Mays, Mickey Mantle, or Duke Snider. But it does include a record five for Lou Gehrig and two each by Sammy Sosa and Todd Helton—the only postwar players to do it twice.

0 Major-league games for Joe Bauman. A feared slugger in the minors, the 6'5", 237-pound lefty hitter won a Triple Crown,

THE BROTHERS
DiMaggio

Image Credit: Ronnie Joyner

0 Although there were three of them, the DiMaggios did not set the record for home runs by brothers. Dom (glasses), Vince (Boston uniform), and Joe (bottom right) each spent at least a decade in the majors, showcasing various skill levels.

hit 337 homers in seven seasons, and compiled a .700 slugging percentage. He even had a 72-homer season. Bauman averaged 50 homers per 150 games—one every 8.6 at-bats—but left the game at 34 because every big-league team thought he was too old to be a prospect.

0 Star sluggers with homers in their first two at-bats. The only men who did that were hardly stars. Bob Nieman of the 1951 St. Louis Browns and Keith McDonald of the 2000 St. Louis Cardinals did not make lasting impressions. The former hit 123 more homers in 3,450 at-bats while the latter went only 3-for-7—with all hits home runs—over his entire career.

Image Credit: Ronnie Joyner

0 Players with more World Series rings than Yogi Berra. The three-time American League MVP led the Yankees to 10 world championships during his 18-year tenure as the team's catcher. He later teased fellow Hall of Famer Derek Jeter that he was twice as good as the shortstop, who "only" won five.

0 Midgets (to use the language at the time) permitted to play baseball after Bill Veeck hired Eddie Gaedel and sent him up to hit in a 1951 game. Commissioner Ford Frick nullified his contract.

0 Brooklyn hitters with 40 homers before Gil Hodges. The Hall of Fame first baseman hit 40 homers, then a Dodgers club record, in 1951.

0 At-bats for Pee Wee Reese in the 1951 All-Star Game. Selected for the fifth year in a row, the Brooklyn shortstop waited on the bench behind Alvin Dark of the Giants. Reese entered the game late but did not get to hit.

Image Credit: Ronnie Joyner

0 Games won by Ralph Branca in 1951 NL playoffs. The Dodgers starter lost Game 1 of the best-of-three pennant playoff as a starter and Game 3 as a ninth-inning reliever who yielded Bobby Thomson's three-run "shot heard 'round the world." Thomson also hit a decisive homer in the opener against Branca, who wore No. 13.

0 Thirty-homer seasons by Hank Aaron during his first three years in the majors. The future home run king didn't break the 30-homer plateau until his fourth season.

0 Fifty-homer seasons for Hank Aaron in his career. A model of consistency, he had a single-season peak of 47 en route to his career total of 755.

0 Teammates who homered more often than Hank Aaron and Eddie Mathews. The Braves sluggers not only hit a record 863 home runs during the time they were teammates, 1954 to 1966, but also homered in the same game 75 times, another major-league record. Both are in Cooperstown.

EDDIE GAEDEL

Image Credit: Ronnie Joyner

0 Official at-bats for Eddie Gaedel. In the second game of a doubleheader on August 19, 1951, the St. Louis Browns inserted Gaedel as a pinch-hitter to lead off the last of the first inning. At 3'7" tall, the 60-pound Gaedel immediately became the shortest player in baseball history. Wearing 1/8 on the back of his uniform, he drew a four-pitch walk from Detroit pitcher Bob Cain, then was lifted for a pinch-runner. Bill Veeck's publicity stunt went unappreciated by higher authorities and American League president Will Harridge voided his contract. Gaedel left with a career on-base percentage of 1.000—the highest possible.

0 Rating Jimmy Piersall gave Anthony Perkins for portraying him in *Fear Strikes Out*, a 1957 film about the outfielder's struggles with mental health. Piersall, later a broadcaster, was diagnosed as a manic depressive with bipolar disorder.

0 Home runs for Nellie Fox in 1958. The spray-hitting White Sox second baseman had 612 at-bats that year but connected in the very first game a year later, ending a 14-inning game with a two-run shot against Detroit's Don Mossi, 9–7.

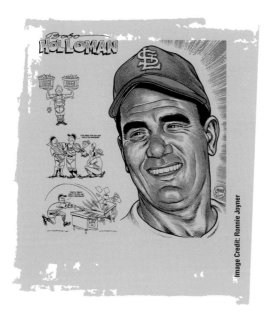

Image Credit: Ronnie Joyner

0 Pitchers before Bobo Holloman with no-hitters in their first start. A Georgia farm boy with the St. Louis Browns, Holloman had no trouble holding the Philadelphia Athletics hitless on May 6, 1953. It was his only shutout and complete game, as arm trouble intervened and short-circuited his career. He was out of the majors within two years.

0 Games Roy Campanella played for the Los Angeles Dodgers. The star Brooklyn backstop had his career cut short by a winter car crash that left him paralyzed before the team transferred to Los Angeles for the 1958 season.

0 Home runs by Carroll Hardy as a regular in 1958. He had just one home run that year—while pinch-hitting for future home run king Roger Maris.

0 Left-handed catchers in the majors for four decades. Between Dale Long in 1958 and Mike Squires in 1980, no left-handed catcher played major-league baseball.

0 Years Yankees leadoff man Bobby Richardson scored 100 runs. Though Junior Gilliam routinely scored 100 for the Dodgers, Richardson never reached that plateau.

0 Desire by Ernie Banks to play in the majors. He said he was having such a good time with the Kansas City Monarchs that he wanted to stay in the Negro Leagues.

0 National Leaguers with consecutive MVPs before Ernie Banks. He was the first to win the trophy two years in a row, in 1958 and 1959, even though his Chicago Cubs finished fifth both years and his competition included Hank Aaron, Eddie Mathews, and Willie Mays.

0 Games Ernie Banks played shortstop after moving to first. The two-time National League MVP moved across the diamond after a 1962 knee injury and never returned to his original position.

Image Credit: Ronnie Joyner

0 Hits allowed by Lew Burdette on August 18, 1960. On that date, the Milwaukee Braves' right-hander handcuffed the Philadelphia Phillies for the only no-hitter of his career. The two-time All-Star finished with 203 wins, same as Hall of Famer Roy Halladay, and a World Series MVP award (for his 3–0 record and 0.67 ERA against the New York Yankees in 1957).

Banks had played 717 consecutive games, all at short, before shifting at age 30. He wound up playing only 134 fewer games at short than at first base.

0 Grand slams by Roger Maris in 1961. He hit 61 home runs, a new single-season mark, but none with the bases full.

0 Sunday night games before 1963. The Houston Colt .45s, hoping to help their hitters beat the excessive heat in Texas, played the first Sunday night game on June 9, 1963. Houston won, 3–0, behind Turk Farrell and Hal (Skinny) Brown.

Shantz

Image Credit: Ronnie Joyner

0 Smaller pitchers than Bobby Shantz. A little lefty who measured 5'6" and 139 pounds, Shantz was shunned by Philadelphia A's manager Connie Mack until several veteran pitchers got injured. Given a chance, Shantz responded, eventually winning 24 games and an MVP award in 1952. He lasted 16 seasons, winning 116 games as a combination starter and reliever.

0 Major leaguers with the same first name as 1965 American League MVP Zoilo Versalles, whose nickname was Zorro.

0 Players with 100 steals in a season before World War II. Maury Wills became the first when he swiped 104, breaking Ty Cobb's record of 96, in 1962.

0 First digit of the career batting average by Sandy Koufax. He hit .097 lifetime in a career that ended in 1966.

0 National Leaguers with two grand slams in a game before 1966. Tony Cloninger, a Braves pitcher, did it on July 3, 1966, when he also had an RBI single in a 17–3 romp over San Francisco. Four American League sluggers, led by Tony Lazzeri in 1936, had preceded him.

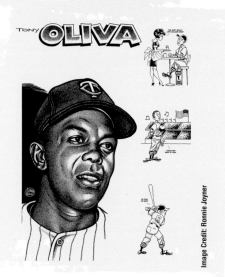

TONY OLIVA

Image Credit: Ronnie Joyner

0 World championships won by Tony Oliva during a 15-year career spent exclusively with the Minnesota Twins. He also remains the only player to win batting crowns in each of his first two full seasons (1964 and 1965).

0 Hitters before Willie McCovey with 45 intentional walks in a year. The Hall of Fame first baseman did that in 1969 but Barry Bonds, later with the same Giants, had more: 68 in 2002, 61 in 2003, and a whopping 120 in 2004, when he finished with a record 232 bases on balls. Babe Ruth was the only other player to walk at least 170 times (in 1923).

0 Players before Dick Allen with multiple inside-the-park homers in a game. He did it during his MVP season with the Chicago White Sox in 1972, connecting twice against Minnesota's Bert Blyleven.

0 Home runs hit by Rod Carew when he won his second batting crown. He hit a league-leading .318 for the Minnesota Twins in 1972 but never hit the ball over the fence.

0 Errors charged to Bill North, whose misjudged fly in the ninth cost Ken Holtzman a no-hitter. Two outs, ninth inning, and a lazy fly ball seemed like a harmless combination—until North went south while trying to catch it. That cost Holtzman, who threw two others, a no-hitter against Detroit on June 9, 1975.

0 Game-winning grand slams for Don Money. His apparent ninth-inning slam helped the Brewers beat the Yankees, 10–9, on April 10, 1976, but umpires ruled that Yankees first baseman Chris Chambliss had called time before the pitch. Forced to bat again, Money hit a fly ball and Milwaukee lost, 9–7.

0 Home runs in 1,593 career at-bats before Frank Taveras finally connected in 1977.

0 Players with two pinch-slams in a season before Davey Johnson. The slugging infielder and future manager did it in 1978.

0 Days spent in the minors by Dave Winfield. He's the only Hall of Famer who went directly to the majors from college after the 1965 advent of the amateur draft.

0 Players other than Rickey Henderson with triple digits in steals and double digits in homers during the same season. Henderson had 130 steals in 1982 and hit 10 home runs that season. He had 297 homers during a career that lasted 25 years.

0 Men with 40-homer seasons in both leagues before Darrell Evans. The lefty-hitting infielder did it for the Atlanta Braves and Detroit Tigers.

0 Hawaii home runs by the San Diego Padres. They failed to homer during a three-game set against the Cardinals in April 1997 but St. Louis slugger Ron Gant did manage to connect. He remains the only major leaguer to hit an official home run in the 50th state.

0 All-Star invites for Kirk Gibson. He was a National League MVP and an American League Championship Series MVP but never an All-Star.

0 Players before 1986 with 100+ steals three years in a row. Vince Coleman did it in his first three seasons, 1986 to 1988.

0 Home runs for the stolen-base champ. Vince Coleman swiped a league-best 107 bases for the St. Louis Cardinals in 1986 but did not hit a single home run.

0 Don Mattingly grand slams except for the year he set a record for grand slams. The Yankees first baseman hit a record six home runs with the bases loaded—and even one during spring training—in 1987 but never hit one before or after in his 14-year career. Mattingly's single-season mark has since been tied by Travis Hafner.

0 Home runs over eight seasons but seven in one. Pitcher Mike Hampton did that in 2001, delivering for the Colorado Rockies with his bat as well as his arm.

0 Times Alfredo Griffin appeared in perfect games his team won. But the shortstop was on teams that lost perfect games *three times*, a dubious way to get into the record book.

0 Players with 40-40 seasons before World War II. The first time it happened was 1988, when Jose Canseco of the Oakland A's had 42 homers and 40 steals for the Oakland A's. Barry Bonds became the first National Leaguer to do it in 1996.

0 Home runs by Ozzie Canseco. The twin brother of Jose, who hit 462, did not share his baseball ability. His entire career lasted 24 games.

0 Ken Holtzman hits in 1974 season. In the second year of the DH, then used only by the American League, the Oakland pitcher did not bat during the regular season. But he did deliver a double and home run in the winning World Series against the Dodgers. He also had a pair of doubles in the World Series the previous year.

0 Home runs on 3-0 count hit by Mark McGwire during 70-homer season. A selective slugger, he did that in 1989.

0 Players with five straight 50-homer seasons. Mark McGwire was the first to do it four times in a row, the major-league record. He won four home run crowns, two in each league.

0 Players before 1996 who led off three straight games with home runs. Baltimore outfielder Brady Anderson did it first, followed by Ronald Acuña Jr. twenty-two years later.

0 Players with batting crowns in four different decades. George Brett led the American League in 1976, 1980, and 1990.

0 Catchers before Sandy Alomar Jr. to start an All-Star Game and win both a Gold Glove and Rookie of the Year. The six-time All-Star filled that void when he did that for Cleveland in 1990.

0 National Leaguers who won home run crowns with three different teams. Reggie Jackson, a career American Leaguer, did it with the Athletics, Yankees, and Angels.

Image Credit: Ronnie Joyner

0 Players before Dave Kingman who performed in four different divisions in one season. An all-or-nothing hitter whose resume includes two home run crowns, Kingman began 1977 with the New York Mets but later moved to the San Diego Padres, California Angels, and New York Yankees—becoming the first man to play in each of the divisions in the same season (three-division play began in 1994).

0 Players with 13 walkoff homers. The major-league record is 12 by Hall of Famer Jim Thome.

0 Players with four RBIs in four-homer games before Mike Cameron. When he connected four times on May 2, 2002, he kept hitting solo shots.

0 Players who homered for their 3,000th hit before Wade Boggs. And he wasn't even a power hitter.

0 Batting crowns by Eddie Murray. The switch-hitting Hall of Famer had 3,255 hits, including 504 homers, during a 21-year career in which he hit .287. But his best bid for a batting crown, a career-peak .330 average in 1990, fell short when Willie McGee won the NL title with a .335 mark—compiled before his move from St. Louis to Oakland at the trade deadline. McGee hit .274 for the A's, bringing his overall mark down to .324, sixth in the majors, but he had enough NL at-bats to claim the crown. Murray's average was actually one point ahead of American League leader George Brett's .329.

0 Amateurs drafted ahead of Chipper Jones. A shortstop who later moved to third base, the switch-hitting slugger was the over-all first pick in the 1990 amateur draft by the Atlanta Braves.

0 NL switch-hitters with a 50-homer season. Chipper Jones and Lance Berkman had 45 each, tops in the National League but well behind Mickey Mantle's 56.

0 Players other than Todd Helton with consecutive 400-total bases seasons. The Colorado first baseman was the only man to do that.

Image Credit: Ronnie Joyner

0 Catchers with three batting crowns before Joe Mauer. The top pick in the 2001 amateur draft, he endeared himself to fans in Minnesota, where he spent his entire 15-year career and led the AL in hitting three times—a first for a catcher. The Twins also gave away Joe Mauer stick-on sideburns during several Target Field promotions.

0 Times Deion Sanders played baseball and football on the same day. It almost happened in 1992, when he played one game for the Atlanta Falcons of the NFL and made it to Pittsburgh in time to play NLCS Game 5 for the Atlanta Braves against the Pirates. But Deion never got into that game.

0 World Series MVP awards given to designated hitters until 1993. In the first 20 years of the DH rule, none was ever voted Most Valuable Player of the World Series. Paul Molitor of the Toronto Blue Jays was the first in 1993.

0 Probability Ripken's record ever falls. Cal Ripken Jr.'s streak of 2,632 consecutive games played between 1982 and 1998 not

Image Credit: Ronnie Joyner

0 Players with 20 World Series home runs. Mickey Mantle hit 18, more than anyone else, while playing in 12 World Series, all with the New York Yankees, starting in 1951.

only broke Lou Gehrig's long-standing mark for longevity but is more than double Steve Garvey's NL mark.

0 Players other than Mike Greenwell with all nine RBIs in 9-run game. The Boston Red Sox outfielder knocked in every Red Sox run against Seattle on September 2, 1996.

0 NL batting champs with four straight titles between 1926 and 1997. After Rogers Hornsby got his fourth in a row, no National Leaguer did it again until Tony Gwynn in 1997. The two men share the league record of eight batting titles, four behind Ty Cobb's major-league mark.

0 Rookies with 88 extra-base hits before Albert Pujols. The Cardinals first baseman did it in 2001.

0 Players before Kevin Kouzmanoff with a grand slam on the first pitch he saw in the majors. He did that in 2006.

0 National Leaguers with an inside-the-park home run in an All-Star Game. The only one in the game's history was produced in San Francisco by Ichiro, star player of the American League's Seattle Mariners, in 2007.

0 Players before Hideki Matsui to win World Series MVP awards without ever playing in the field. In 2009, the Yankees' DH became the first man to do that.

0 Players who spent more than 20 years with the Yankees. Derek Jeter, who played 20 years in the majors, and Mariano Rivera, who played 19, both spent their whole careers in pinstripes. Nobody played for the Yankees longer than the two future Hall of Famers.

0 Live introductions for post-2010 Derek Jeter at-bats in Yankee Stadium. After the passing of long-term public address announcer Bob Sheppard, Yankees captain Derek Jeter asked that recordings of Sheppard's voice be played when he came to bat. Jeter retired after the 2014 season, his 20th with the Yankees.

0 Twentieth-century players with six RBIs in their first game. Starlin Castro of the Chicago Cubs became the first on May 7, 2010, leading a 14–7 win over Cincinnati. He had a three-run homer in his first at-bat and a triple with the bases loaded later.

0 Hall of Famers before Frank Thomas to play more than half their games as a designated hitter. Thomas, inducted in 2014, was a first baseman who spent his later years as a DH.

0 Players who hit more than 25 grand slam home runs. Alex Rodriguez hit the most, with 25 of his 696 career home runs occurring with the bases loaded.

0 National Leaguers with multiple two-homer innings. American League star Alex Rodriguez was the only player to do that.

Image Credit: Ronnie Joyner

0 Most Valuable Player awards won by Derek Jeter. The Yankee captain, a 14-time All-Star who spent his entire 20-year career with the Yankees, won American League Rookie of the Year honors and Most Valuable Player trophies in the All-Star Game and World Series. But he never won an MVP for the regular season.

0 Room for A-Rod in 700-home run club. The long-time Yankees slugger fell four short, finishing with 696, because of a year-long PED suspension late in his career.

0 Navajo players in baseball before Jacoby Ellsbury. The fleet outfielder was the first from Navajo nation.

0 Batting crowns for Melky Cabrera. When suspended for using steroids during the 2012 season, he was one plate appearance shy of the minimum number needed to qualify. But he asked the Players Association to ignore Rule 10.22 (a) and give the title to

0 Days Alex Rodriguez spent on the Yankees roster at the start of the 2009 season. The slugging infielder was sidelined after hip surgery but returned earlier than expected, slamming a three-run homer in his first game, against the Baltimore Orioles, on May 8. He finished with a 30-homer, 100-RBI campaign that helped New York win its 27th world championship.

Image Credit: Ronnie Joyner

teammate Buster Posey, hitting 10 points less. Cabrera did not return the All-Star MVP trophy he won that summer, however.

0 Batting titles by Astros before Jose Altuve. The diminutive second baseman won one in 2014.

0 Non-Cubs infielders in the 2015 NL All-Star infield. Cubs fans stuffed the ballot box, electing Kris Bryant, Javy Baez, Ben Zobrist, and Anthony Rizzo.

0 World Series appearances for Raul Mondesi. He played 1,525 games but never made it, while son Raul A. Mondesi made the World Series in 2015 *before playing in his first official game.*

0 Players before 2016 who got their first hit of the season in the World Series. Kyle Schwarber of the Cubs not only became the first but hit .412 (7-for-17) as a DH and pinch-hitter for the victorious Chicago Cubs against the Cleveland Indians. It was Chicago's first world title since 1908.

0 Official at-bats for Bryce Harper on May 8, 2016. He had seven plate appearances in the Mother's Day game for the Nationals against the Cubs but drew six walks—three of them intentional—and was hit by a pitch. In the four-game series, he reached base 12 consecutive times without an at-bat.

0 Number of months in which Scooter Gennett had four homers before he hit four in a game. The least likely member of the four home run club, Gennett joined on June 6, 2017, when he hit four in a game for the Reds against the Cardinals.

0 Hits by Ron Wright. His whole career consisted of three at-bats in which he made six outs: a strikeout, a double play, and a triple-play.

0 Twentieth-century players to win world championship, MVP award, Gold Glove, and Silver Slugger in the same season. The first man to do it was Mookie Betts of the 2018 Boston Red Sox.

0 Braves with more leadoff homers than Ronald Acuña Jr. The Venezuelan outfielder hit a club-record eight of his 26 home runs as a rookie from the leadoff spot in 2018.

0 Cycles for Ichiro Suzuki. The single-season hits leader and member of the 3,000-hit club never hit a single, double, triple, and home run in the same game. Neither did any other Japanese native until Shohei Ohtani in 2019.

0 Number of times Ichiro stole home. He played 19 years but never did that, though he did pitch once.

0 Players before Ichiro with six straight 200-hit seasons.

0 Previous players comparable to Shohei Ohtani. The 2021 American League MVP, Ohtani had an unprecedented season as a two-way star. He hit 46 homers and allowed the exact same number of runs. He had 80 extra-base hits, 26 stolen bases, a 9–2 pitching record, 3.18 earned run average, and 156 strikeouts in 130 1/3 innings pitched. Ohtani, 27, can be a free agent for the first time after the 2023 season.

0 *Players* before Ohtani who batted first, served as starting pitcher, and got the win in the same game. When Shohei Ohtani did it in the 2021 All-Star Game in Denver, it was the first time any player ever turned that trick—even in a regular-season game.

0 Players of the Live Ball Era's first century with 10 homers and 10 wins in a season. Shohei Ohtani became the first man to do it but in 2021–101 years after the start of the Live Ball Era.

0 NL pitchers who hit 40 home runs. Shohei Ohtani, used as a pitcher and designated hitter by the Los Angeles Angels in 2021, hit 46 home runs. Wes Ferrell held the previous American League record with 38 *lifetime* home runs, three more than National League leader Warren Spahn.

0 American League players of the DH era who stole home and started a game as a pitcher in the same season. Since the American League introduced the designated hitter in 1973, nobody stole home and started a game until Shohei Ohtani on August 31, 2021.

0 Cincinnati players with multiple 3-homer games in a season before 2021. Jesse Winker did it twice that year and was "rewarded" with an offseason trade to Seattle by the cost-cutting Reds.

0 Paternal tandems with MVP awards. In 2021, Vladimir Guerrero Jr. was MVP runner-up to Shohei Ohtani, making the Guerreros the first paternal tandem to finish in the top two for any major award.

0 Designated hitters with 500 home runs. David (Big Papi) Ortiz, a 2022 Hall of Fame inductee, hit a record 485 as a DH, mostly with the Boston Red Sox.

0 Players with cycles in both regular season and postseason. Atlanta's Eddie Rosario came close in 2021 when he hit for the cycle in August and then had a postseason game with two homers, a triple, and a single.

0 Cycles in All-Star history. Willie Mays came close, with a single, double, and triple in the 1960 game at Kansas City, then collected three more hits in the second All-Star Game at Yankee Stadium.

0 Players with three cycles in a season. Babe Ruth, Aaron Hill, and Christian Yelich had two, with Yelich producing against the same team: Cincinnati. Yelich, the 2018 NL MVP, later had a record third career cycle against the Reds.

0 Players who hit 10 triples in 2021. It was the first season in baseball history that no one hit that many.

0 Number of times Victor Robles went from first to third on a single in 2021. The normally speedy Washington outfielder was 0-for-14 in such opportunities.

0 Number of times Mike Piazza or Keith Hernandez had multiple walk-off RBIs for the Mets in a season. A rookie catcher named Patrick Mazeika had two in 2021 before he even got his first hit. Both came on fielder's choices.

0 Triples by Pete Alonso in his first 1,156 trips to the plate. When he finally hit one, on August 16, 2021, it ended a record streak of 68 games without a triple *by the entire Mets team.*

0 Career homers for Seby Zavala before he hit three in a game. His surprising outburst came on July 31, 2021, for the Chicago White Sox.

0 Grand slams by Pete Alonso when he set the rookie home run record. In 2019, none of his record 53 home runs came with the bases loaded. In fact, the Mets first baseman hit 106 before his first grand slam, which came in his third season, on April 9, 2022.

0 National League MVPs from the New York Mets. Three players from the 1962 National League expansion franchise managed to finish second in the voting: Keith Hernandez, Darryl Strawberry, and Tom Seaver.

0 Players with four grand slams in 19 days. Light-hitting Tampa Bay utilityman Brett Phillips came closest with three slams and an inside-the-park shot between July 26 and August 16, 2021. That topped a similar showing by Babe Ruth that required 36 days, the previous record. Between July 29 and August 11, Phillips hit three slams in 19 plate appearances, second only to Jim Northrup, who needed just 14 appearances in 1968. On August 16, Phillips hit an inside-the-park home run but not with the bases loaded. The combination of three slams and an inside-the-park homer in 19 days broke a record held by Ruth, who needed 36 days for the same feat in 1929.

0 Players before 2022 to reach base 12 times in their first three games. Steven Kwan of the newly named Cleveland Guardians did that in 2022. In his first four games, the outfielder reached base 15 times, a major-league record.

0 Pirates hit by a pitch in April 2022. While New York Mets players were hit 19 times during that month, no Pittsburgh player was plunked.

0 Hits for 40-somethings Albert Pujols and Yadier Molina on 2022 Opening Day. Pujols, 42, and Molina, pushing 40, went a combined 0-for-9 in the Cardinals' opener.

0 April homers for Trey Mancini in 2022. The once-feared slugger struggled mightily after his team, the Baltimore Orioles, moved the left-field barrier at Oriole Park 26 feet further from the plate.

0 Teams with 60 home runs from players not on their Opening Day roster. The world champion Atlanta Braves of 2021 hold the major-league mark with 59, thanks mainly to midseason acquisitions Adam Duvall, Eddie Rosario, Joc Pederson, and Jorge Soler.

0 World Series games for Junior. Griffey, longtime star of the Seattle Mariners, played in 2,671 games without winning a pennant or advancing to the Fall Classic.

0 Days Isiah Kiner-Falefa spent with the Minnesota Twins. Traded by the Texas Rangers early in 2022 after a four-year run at shortstop there, he immediately moved to the New York Yankees in a five-man deal that also brought Josh Donaldson to the Bronx. The deal improved the defense in the Yankees infield,

with Kiner-Falefa solidifying short, Donaldson playing third, and Gleyber Torres returning to second base from shortstop.

0 Older hitters than Buck O'Neil. A Negro Leagues standout who became the first black coach in the majors with the Cubs, he suited up and batted for the Kansas City T-Bones at age 94.

0 Players who hit into five triple plays. Brooks Robinson, who could field but not run, holds this dubious record with four.

0 Players suspended in the Biogenesis scandal for failing a drug test. Thirteen players were named, including Alex Rodriguez and Ryan Braun, in the 2013 scandal.

0 Players before 2022 whose first two hits were multi-run homers. Rookie catcher Brian Serven of the Colorado Rockies was the first to do that.

0 Hits by Chris Davis in 17-inning game. The Baltimore first baseman went 0-for-18 on May 6, 2012, but got some good news out of the game too: he was the winning pitcher after pitching two scoreless innings against the Red Sox.

0 Players who averaged 400 total bases over four years. Starting in 1998, Sammy Sosa had 1,621 total bases over a four-year span, topping Chuck Klein's 69-year-old record of 1,616.

0 Cycles by stars in postseason play. The first man to produce one was Red Sox utilityman Brock Holt, on October 8, 2018, in ALDS Game 4 at Yankee Stadium. Holt had a regular-season cycle too: against the Braves on June 16, 2015.

0 Players with 900 home runs. Japanese slugger Sadaharu Oh had 868, most by anyone who played professional baseball, and won 15 home run crowns and nine MVPs in his home country.

0 Runs scored by Red Sox in Roger Maris record-breaker. The solo homer Maris hit on October 1, 1961, not only broke Babe Ruth's single-season record of 60 but was the only run scored in the Red Sox-Yankees game on the final day of the season.

0 Latinos in Cooperstown before Roberto Clemente. The late Pittsburgh star, who lost his life ferrying supplies to Nicaragua after an earthquake, was elected by a special vote in 1973. The first Puerto Rican in the Hall of Fame was also the first Latino.

0 Number of hits Willie Mays got in his first 12 at-bats. Then he homered against Warren Spahn and started to hit.

0 Home runs by future slugger Todd Helton in the Cape Cod League. And he played there for two summers.

0 Stolen bases by Marcell Ozuna during his first two Atlanta seasons. He never stole a base for the Braves in 2020, when he led the National League in home runs and runs batted in, or in 2021, when his season was shortened by injury (fractured fingers) and legal problems (violation of MLB's domestic abuse policies). But that streak of inactivity ended early in the 2022 season.

0 Players with eight pinch-homers in a season. Dave Hansen and Craig Wilson each hit seven, the major-league record.

0 Brother tandems with more home runs than the Aarons. Hank and Tommie combined for 768, a total that topped the Alous, Bells, Boones, DiMaggios, and others.

0 Fathers and sons with more 30-30 years than the Bonds. Bobby and Barry Bonds, who each had five, hold a firm grip on this speed-plus-power record.

0 MVP awards for Big Papi. Although he won a slew of honors for his prodigious slugging, David Ortiz never won the American League's Most Valuable Player Award. He did, however, win the Edgar Martinez Designated Hitter Award eight times, more than any other player.

0 World Series appearances for Nick Markakis. He played a record 2,154 games without reaching the Fall Classic.

0 RBI crowns won by Willie Mays.

Image Credit: Ronnie Joyner

0 Games played in 2021 by Robinson Cano. The second baseman of the New York Mets was banned for the season after a third positive test for performance-enhancing substances.

0 Players from the Murderers Row Yankees to homer in their first at-bat. Earl Averill of the Cleveland Indians was the first major-leaguer to do it, connecting in 1929, two years after the slugging Yankees acquired the Murderers Row nickname.

0 Ron Blomberg home runs against Bert Blyleven. The Hall of Fame control artist and curveball specialist once yielded a record 50 home runs in a season but never allowed a home run to Blomberg, who played seven years for the Yankees after becoming the first DH on April 6, 1973.

0 All-Star Games played in 1945. Wartime travel restrictions intervened.

0 All-Star Games in 2020. The Midsummer Classic was wiped out by COVID-19, a lethal pandemic that shortened the season to 60 games.

0 Exhibition games played in Florida during World War II. During the peak war years of 1943, 1944, and 1945, teams trained close to home because of wartime travel restrictions.

0 AL pitchers with Cy Young and Rookie of the Year awards in the same season. The only man to do that was Fernando Valenzuela, a portly Mexican southpaw, with the 1981 Los Angeles Dodgers.

0 Consecutive multi-homer games for Ernie Banks at Wrigley Field. The man called Mr. Cub hit 512 in his career but never connected twice in a game at home in two straight games—even with the wind blowing out.

0 National League fathers and sons with consecutive home runs. The Griffeys did it for the American League's Seattle Mariners. After Junior joined the varsity in 1989, he and his dad became the first paternal pair to play together. They also were the first with back-to-back homers.

0 Games played by Kendrys Morales in 2011. He sat out the season—and all but 51 games of the previous campaign—after breaking his leg while celebrating a game-winning grand slam by jumping on home plate. It was the most agonizing of his 213 career homers.

0 Games Dave Nilsson played after a mosquito bite. The Milwaukee catcher contracted Ross River Fever in his native Australia during the 1994–95 offseason and missed the first two months of the major-league season in 1995. Nilsson retired after the 1997 campaign.

0 Players with 30 pinch-hits in a season. The record of 28 is owned by John Vander Wal, who did it in 1995.

0 Twentieth-century outfielders with 40 homers, 40 doubles, 40 steals, and 20 assists. Alfonso Soriano was the first to do that, but it didn't happen until 2006.

0 Home runs Hank Aaron hit against the Chicago White Sox. They were the only team not to yield a home run to the man who broke Babe Ruth's career record.

0 Players close to Hank Aaron's record for total bases. Aaron had 6,856, far ahead of runner-up Stan Musial's 6,134.

0 Triple Crowns for Joe DiMaggio. A 13-time All-Star who won nine World Series rings, the Yankee Clipper led the American League in batting, home runs, and runs batted in twice each but never led in all three Triple Crown categories in the same season.

0 Players with better batting averages in Boston than Wade Boggs. The five-time batting king hit a robust .369 at Fenway Park, better than Ted Williams or any other player.

0 Members of the 3,000-hit club to enter with a triple before Paul Molitor. On September 16, 1996, Molitor hit a triple for his 3,000th hit.

0 Numbers retired before Lou Gehrig's. The New York Yankees retired the dying first baseman's number 4 on July 4, 1939, the date he told Yankee Stadium fans he was "the luckiest man on the face of the earth." The Yankees have since retired all of their single-digit uniforms.

0 National Leaguers with nine batting crowns. Rogers Hornsby and Tony Gwynn had eight straight, the NL record. Ty Cobb had 12 in the American League.

0 National Leaguers to win batting crowns in three different decades. George Brett of the Kansas City Royals, an American League team, was the only man to do that.

0 Home runs for Denny McLain after his first game. The two-time Cy Young Award winner hit the only one of his career in his 1963 debut.

0 Double brothers in the same infield outside of Cincinnati. The 1998 Reds completed their season by starting an infield of Aaron Boone, Barry Larkin, Bret Boone, and Stephen Larkin from third to first.

0 Rookies with 50 home runs before Aaron Judge. The towering Yankees outfielder hit 52 in 2017 but his record was short-lived, as Pete Alonso of the Mets followed with 53 two years later.

0 MLB games played by Bill Sharman. The future basketball Hall of Famer was playing in the farm system of the Brooklyn Dodgers when promoted to the majors. On September 27, 1951, he was in the dugout when teammates erupted in anger after a close play and were ejected en masse by umpire Frank Dascoli. Sharman, on the bench, was also tossed and never got into a game.

0 National Leaguers who made unassisted triple plays in the World Series. The only time it happened, in 1920, it was done by Cleveland's Bill Wambsganss.

0 Home runs by Mets position players on May 2, 2019. Pitcher Noah Syndergaard hit the only home run of the game, giving him all the offense he needed to beat Cincinnati, 1–0.

0 MVP trophies for Ted Williams in Triple Crown seasons. Wildly unpopular with voting writers, he lost MVP votes to Joe Gordon in 1942 and Joe DiMaggio in 1949.

0 Players other than Mike Trout with consecutive All-Star MVPs.

Pitchers

0.968 WHIP (walks plus hits per innings pitched) of Hall of Famer Addie Joss. It was the best in baseball history, just edging Mariano Rivera's 1.000.

0 Challengers to Cy Young's record for complete games. The career leader in wins and losses went all the way 749 times. Few pitchers even made that many *appearances*.

0 Phillies 20-game winners between Grover Cleveland Alexander and Robin Roberts. The former won 30 games in 1917, while Roberts finished with 20 when he beat the Brooklyn Dodgers, 4-1, in a 10-inning game that clinched the 1950 National League pennant for the Whiz Kids.

Image Credit: Ronnie Joyner

0 American Leaguers with 30-win seasons after age 30. The only man to do that pitched for a National League team. Joe (Iron Man) McGinnity won 31 games at age 32 and then 35 a year later. The New York Giants star worked 434 innings, still an NL record, in 1903 and was still pitching in the minors well into his fifties.

0 National League pitchers with 400 wins. Although Cy Young won a record 511 games while dividing his time between the two leagues, he did not win 300 games in either. Grover Cleveland Alexander and Christy Mathewson share the National League lead with 373.

0.00 Team ERA of the New York Giants in the 1905 World Series. Aided by a rainout that gave him an unscheduled day of rest, Christy Mathewson blanked the Philadelphia Athletics three times and Joe McGinnity also shut them out. When he pitched another shutout in the 1913 World Series, Big Six became the only man to pitch more than three Series shutouts in his *career*.

0 Runs Jesse Tannehill allowed to break Boston's 20-game losing streak. On May 25, 1906, he throttled the Chicago White Sox, 3–0, to end Boston's streak, which had included 19 straight at home.

0 Runs allowed by Detroit's Ed Summers in an 18-inning game. On July 16, 1909, he allowed seven hits while pitching all 18 innings against Washington in a game that ended in a 0–0 tie.

0 Rookie awards for Grover Cleveland Alexander. He won 28 games for the Phillies in his first major-league season, 1911, but the Rookie of the Year Award was not created until 1947.

0 Pitching tandems with 500 wins. The record is 463 by Christy Mathewson and Hooks Wiltse, a right-left tandem with the New York Giants for 11 years from 1904 to 1914. The team won five pennants during their time as teammates.

0 Single-season pitching tandems with 70 wins. In 1904, Christy Mathewson went 33–12 and Iron Man Joe McGinnity was 35–8, giving them a two-man total of 68 that has never been topped.

0 Wins for Henry Mathewson. Christy's brother pitched in three games for the New York Giants of 1906 and 1907 but never won one. Yet the Mathewsons held the record for most wins by brothers for years before the Perrys and Niekros passed them. Christy had 373 all by himself.

0 Run support for Christy Mathewson and Joe McGinnity on June 7, 1906. The New York Giants aces—both future Hall of Famers—allowed 11 first-inning runs in a 19–0 defeat by the Chicago Cubs.

0 Number worn by Christy Mathewson. During his career in the majors, no teams wore numbers on their jerseys.

Image Credit: Ronnie Joyner

WALTER JOHNSON

0 Pitchers with more shutouts than Walter Johnson. The Big Train, who pitched exclusively for the Washington Senators, won 417 games—a record 110 of them by shutting out his opponents. Only Cy Young had more victories, though not as many shutouts.

0 National Leaguers with 100 shutouts. Walter Johnson, with 110, was the only man to finish with triple digits in that department. Grover Cleveland Alexander has the NL mark with 90.

0 American League lefties with 10 shutouts in a season. Babe Ruth's 1916 record of nine remains the record. Ruth was then pitching for the Boston Red Sox, playing half his games in compact Fenway Park, often regarded as a graveyard for left-handed pitchers because of its short left field.

0 Runs allowed by Babe Ruth vs. Yankees in first game of 1917 season. Then a left-handed starter for the Boston Red Sox, Ruth pitched a three-hit shutout on Opening Day, went on to win

RON NECCIAI

Image Credit: Ronnie Joyner

0 Pitchers other than Ron Necciai with 27 strikeouts in a game. The 19-year-old Pittsburgh Pirates farmhand fanned 27 hitters during a no-hit effort for Bristol of the Appalachian League on May 13, 1952. He allowed four base-runners: on a walk, hit batsman, error, and a passed ball on a third strike. Wracked by stomach ulcers that night, he allowed the opposition Welch Miners to put the ball in play only twice: on two ground balls. He then fanned 24 in his next start. Finally called to the majors, he won only one of seven decisions before injuries ended his career.

23 more games, and led the American League with 35 complete games.

0 Pitchers with 10 ERA titles. Lefty Grove holds the record with nine.

0 Pitchers who faced Babe Ruth and Roger Maris. Nobody faced both Ruth and the man who broke his single-season home run record, but a journeyman named Al Benton came close. He pitched against Ruth, who starred in the '20s and '30s, and Mickey Mantle, a slugger of the '50s and '60s.

0 Number of curveballs Dizzy Dean threw when he said he wouldn't. After announcing he'd win a game for the 1934

Image Credit: Ronnie Joyner

0 Pitchers before Firpo Marberry used as heavy-duty relievers. Marberry, who helped pitch the Washington Senators to consecutive pennants in 1924 and 1925, was the first pitcher employed mainly as a reliever.

Gashouse Gang Cardinals without throwing a single curve, the brash Cardinal did just that, beating the Boston Braves, 3–0.

0 Losses for Carl Hubbell during his record streak. The star southpaw of the New York Giants won 24 games in a row, a major-league record, over two seasons, 1936 and 1937.

0 American League pitchers with consecutive no-hitters. National Leaguer Johnny Vander Meer of the 1938 Cincinnati Reds was the only man to do it.

0 Big-league pitchers other than Bob Feller whose high school graduations were covered by the national media. Feller, signed by Cleveland as a 16-year-old high school sophomore, had his graduation covered by the NBC radio network.

0 Cy Young Awards for Bob Feller. The pitching award was first given in 1956, the year the Cleveland pitching star retired.

0 Hits allowed by Bob Feller on Opening Day 1940. Pitching for the Cleveland Indians, he beat the Chicago White Sox in the only no-hitter pitched in the first game of the season.

0 Run support for Bob Feller against Floyd Giebell. The Detroit rookie pitched a 2–0 shutout against Feller's Indians to clinch the 1940 AL pennant by one game. Giebell won just two other games during his short-lived stay in the majors.

0 Dazzy Vance wins before age 30. He's the only Hall of Famer to get all of his victories (197) after his 30th birthday.

0 Luck with mules by Bobo Newsom. The pitcher broke both legs in a car crash, then had a mishap the day his casts were removed: attending a South Carolina mule auction, he broke a leg again when a mule kicked him.

0 Wartime weather announcements by Dizzy Dean. Barred from reporting weather conditions by World War II restrictions, the pitcher-turned-broadcaster told his listeners, "I can't tell you why this game is being delayed, but if you really want to know, look out your window."

0 Times Lefty Grove's number was retired. For reasons unknown, neither the A's nor the Red Sox retired the No. 10 of the 300-game winner.

Image Credit: Ronnie Joyner

0 Number of his former St. Louis Browns teammates active when Don Larsen retired. The last active player from the team that became the Baltimore Orioles in 1955, Larsen hung up his spikes in 1967. He remains the only man to author a perfect game in the World Series (for the 1956 New York Yankees).

0 Defeats as a starter for the rookie Satchel Paige. Snatched out of the Negro Leagues by Bill Veeck, the legendary pitcher was at least 42 when added to the Cleveland Indians varsity in 1948. Used as both a reliever and starter by playing manager Lou Boudreau, he went 4–0 in seven starts, throwing two complete-game shutouts and helping the Indians win the pennant by one game over the Boston Red Sox. Paige finished with a 6–1 record and 2.48 ERA.

0 Pitchers with 500 strikeouts in a season. While Nolan Ryan holds the Modern Era major-league record with 383, a minor-leaguer had nearly 100 more. Bill Kennedy fanned 456 in 280 innings for Rocky Mount in the Coastal Plains League in 1946. The left-hander went 28–3 with a 1.03 ERA and 14.7 strikeouts per nine innings. He eventually played eight years in the majors but fell victim to arm problems and wound up 15–28 with a 4.71 ERA.

0 Complete games for Bobo Holloman after a no-hitter. The St. Louis Browns pitcher held the Philadelphia Athletics hitless, winning 6–0 on May 6, 1953, in his first major-league start, but never went the route again. Tyler Gilbert of the Arizona Diamondbacks also hurled a no-hitter in his starting debut, in 2021.

0 Years Warren Spahn had 200 strikeouts. He still managed to win three NL strikeout crowns.

0 Major awards missed by Don Newcombe. The big Brooklyn right-hander was National League Rookie of the Year and Most Valuable Player before winning the newly-created Cy Young Award in 1956.

0 Perfect games at Yankee Stadium before Don Larsen. The first one in the history of the storied Bronx ballpark, which opened in 1923, was Larsen's perfect game against the Brooklyn Dodgers in the 1956 World Series. Larsen and batterymate Yogi Berra, at the stadium to throw out the first pitch on July 18, 1999, must have inspired David Cone, who threw the second regular-season perfect game in the Bronx, against the Montreal Expos, that same day. David Wells pitched the first one a year earlier.

0 American League pitchers who started All-Star Games in three different decades. The only one to do that was Warren Spahn of the Boston/Milwaukee Braves, a National League franchise.

0 National Leaguers with World Series wins in three different decades. The only man to win World Series games in three different decades was career American Leaguer Jim Palmer of the Baltimore Orioles.

0 Relievers needed for Robin Roberts. The future Hall of Famer once pitched 28 consecutive complete games for the Philadelphia Phillies.

0 Losses by Lew Burdette in the 1957 World Series. He went 3–0 with two shutouts, leading the Milwaukee Braves to an upset world title in seven games. He worked the finale on short rest after Warren Spahn came down with the flu.

0 Runs allowed by Juan Marichal in his debut. The high-kicking San Francisco right-hander one-hit the Phillies, 2–0, on July 19, 1960.

0 Pitchers who hit 155 batters. Dodgers sidearmer Don Drysdale, often called a head-hunter, plunked 154, the major-league record, during a career that spanned 22 seasons. Orlando Cepeda once said of him, "The trick is to hit Drysdale before he hits you."

0 Pitchers with six straight ERA titles. Had he not retired with arthritis at age 30, Sandy Koufax might have done it. In his final five years, he won five straight ERA crowns—still the major-league record—while going 111–34 and pitching four no-hitters, the most by a National Leaguer. Koufax even went out with a bang, winning his fourth Cy Young in his final season.

0 AL pitchers with ERA titles in three decades. Only Warren Spahn, a career National Leaguer, did that, leading the NL in 1947, 1953, and 1961.

0 Hits by Cubs pitcher Bob Buhl in 1962, when he went 0-for-70, the worst one-year performance by any major-league player before or since.

0 First digit of Bob Buhl's career batting average. A very good right-handed pitcher who had a knack for beating the Dodgers and finished with a career record of 166–132, Buhl was a bigger bust at bat than Venus de Milo. Playing for the Braves, Cubs, and Phillies, he had a lifetime average of .089.

0 Pitchers before 1968 to sweep MVP awards. In the Year of the Pitcher, Bob Gibson of the Cardinals took National League honors while Denny McLain of the Tigers won the AL honor.

0 Home runs for Gaylord Perry over his first seven seasons. Giants manager Alvin Dark said in 1962 that there would be a man on the moon before Perry hit a home run. Sure enough, Gaylord homered on July 20, 1969, the day of the lunar landing, and proceeded to hit seven more home runs before he hung up his spikes. He and brother Jim won three games between them on the day of the lunar moonwalk.

0 Rookie All-Star Game starting pitchers before 1962. Dave Stenhouse of the Washington Senators was the first.

0 Major-league innings for Larry Yount. Called in to pitch for the 1971 Houston Astros, the brother of two-time MVP Robin Yount injured his shoulder on his first warm-up pitch and never appeared on a major-league mound again.

0 Relief records Mike Marshall didn't break. In 1974, the durable Dodgers right-hander worked 106 games and 208 innings, all in relief, and won the National League's Cy Young Award. In the offseason, he taught kinesiology—the science of muscle movement in relation to body tissue—at Michigan State University.

0 Pitchers who yielded four straight homers before 1963. That's when Detroit's Paul Foytack found his 15 minutes of fame (or ignominy). Others in this dubious club are Chase Wright, Dave Bush, Michael Blazek, Craig Stammen, Roel Ramirez, and Kyle Gibson.

0 Complete games by Dick Radatz. Used exclusively in relief by the Boston Red Sox, "The Monster" was a big guy with a flaming fastball.

0 Pitchers between 1967 and 2021 to no-hit opponents into the eighth inning of a World Series game. Jim Lonborg of the Red Sox went 7 2/3 innings in Game 2 of the '67 Series against the Cardinals before Ian Anderson, A. J. Minter, and Luke Jackson of the Braves threw seven hitless frames in Game 3 of the 2021 Fall Classic against the Astros. Anderson was the first pitcher since Christy Mathewson from 1905 to 1911 to limit opponents to two or fewer runs in his first five postseason starts.

0 Pitchers who won 30 games between 1934 and 1968. Nobody did it between Dizzy Dean of the '34 Cardinals and Denny McLain of the '68 Tigers.

0 Players who gave organ lessons for $3.50 a session. Denny McLain was the first.

0 Pitching brothers with more wins than the Niekros. Phil and Joe combined for 538, 10 more than Gaylord and Jim Perry, for the major-league record.

0 Pitchers with 40-save seasons in both leagues before Jeff Reardon.

0 Mets no-hitters for Tom Seaver, Nolan Ryan, and Doc Gooden. All pitched no-hitters after they left.

0 Games Jim Palmer pitched for the Royals. The Baltimore Orioles left the future Hall of Famer exposed in the 1968 expansion draft but neither new team—the Kansas City Royals nor Seattle Pilots—drafted him. Palmer pitched exclusively for Baltimore.

Image Credit: Ronnie Joyner

0 Number of dissenting votes when Mariano Rivera was elected to the Baseball Hall of Fame. He remains the only player chosen unanimously.

0 Pitchers who threw no-hit games at Forbes Field. The home park of the Pirates from 1909 to 1970, Forbes never hosted a no-hitter.

0 Brothers tandems with no-hitters before 1979. That's the year Houston's Ken Forsch pitched his family into the record books with a hitless game against the Braves. Brother Bob had no-hit the Phillies a year earlier for the Cardinals.

0 AL pitchers who were Rookie of the Year and Cy Young Award winners in the same season. The only man ever to do that was Fernando Valenzuela of the 1981 Dodgers, a National League team.

0 No-hitters by Seattle Mariners before 1990. The American League expansion franchise did not have a no-hit game until Randy Johnson blanked the Detroit Tigers, 2–0, on June 2, 1990. The 6'10" southpaw walked six and fanned eight en route to the first no-hitter in the Kingdome, which opened for baseball in 1977, the same year the Mariners began play.

0 World Series MVPs for Bruce Hurst. Writers had just voted the Red Sox pitcher the trophy for the 1986 World Series when the Mets spoiled the party by winning Game 6 with two outs in the bottom of the tenth inning and then winning again two nights later. The Hurst award was rescinded and given to New York's Ray Knight instead.

0 Hits yielded by Andy Hawkins in defeat. He pitched a no-hitter against the White Sox in 1990 but lost when his Yankees yielded four unearned runs, thanks to three errors in the eighth inning.

0 Wins for Anthony Young in 29 decisions as a starter. Between April 9, 1992, when he pitched for the Mets, and May 6, 1994, with the Cubs, Young went more than two years without a win in a game he started. The 29-game losing streak was a major-league record for futility.

0 Games pitched by Mariano Rivera outside pinstripes. The Colorado Rockies and Miami Marlins could have selected the future star closer from the New York Yankees in the 1992 expansion draft but didn't. Rivera eventually spent his entire 19-year career with the Yanks.

0 Cy Young Awards for Mariano Rivera, who saved a record 652 games and became the lone Hall of Famer elected by unanimous vote.

0 Players with a .400 lifetime batting average. Of all players who appeared in at least 500 games, pitcher Terry Forster came closest. The rotund left-handed reliever hit .397 and was often used as a pinch-hitter by the Chicago White Sox.

0 Injuries to Max Fried during an LA earthquake. Born in Santa Monica Hospital less than 24 hours before the 6.7 Northridge quake that caused $20 billion damage in 1994, baby Max and family were safely evacuated from the hospital because officials feared it might collapse.

0 Philip Humber complete games following his perfect game for the Chicago White Sox at Seattle on April 7, 2012. He finished his career with a lifetime earned run average of 6.44.

BEHOLD THE POWER OF THE "K"!

Image Credit: Ronnie Joyner

0 Roger Clemens sons without the first initial K. The seven-time Cy Young Award winner, who twice fanned 20 men in a nine-inning game, used the letter K—the scorer's symbol for strikeout —in naming his four sons Koby, Kory, Kacy, and Kody.

0 Number of times Greg Maddux fanned Tony Gwynn. The longtime San Diego star had 107 plate appearances against the star right-hander.

0 World Series MVP awards won by Greg Maddux. His left-handed pitching partner with the Braves, Tom Glavine, won the coveted award in 1995.

0 Complete games by WS MVP Tom Glavine in 1995 Fall Classic. The crafty Braves lefty beat the Cleveland Indians twice and had a one-hit shutout over eight innings in the decisive Game 6 before Mark Wohlers finished up. Glavine had a 1.29 ERA while working 14 innings over two starts. In his career, he had 25 complete-game shutouts, including two in difficult Denver, but that total was nearly half of his career total of 56 complete games.

Image Credit: Ronnie Joyner

0 No-hitters thrown by Greg Maddux. But he remains the living pitcher with the most wins (355).

Image Credit: Ronnie Joyner

0 Hits allowed by Tom Glavine during the first five innings of the 1995 World Series finale. The Atlanta lefty yielded a bloop single by Tony Peña to start the sixth, then left after eight innings with a 1-0 lead. The Braves won the game and he was voted World Series MVP.

Image Credit: Ronnie Joyner

0 Pitchers with 420 strikeouts before Virgil Trucks. The rookie right-hander fanned 420, a new professional baseball record, in the 1938 Alabama-Florida League. He had four no-hitters in the minors and two in the majors—both for the 1952 Detroit Tigers.

0 Braves pitchers who won the Warren Spahn Award. Named for the great Braves left-hander, the award has never gone to a Braves lefty since its inception in 1999.

0 Career hits by Jack Morris. The Hall of Fame pitcher scored four runs as a pinch-runner and even got four at-bats in National League parks. But the DH otherwise blocked his path to the plate, as he spent his entire career in the AL.

0 Strikeout crowns for Don Sutton. He had 3,574 career strikeouts while pitching in both leagues. He won 324 games but never fanned more than 217 in a season.

0 Home runs by Don Sutton. The pitcher holds the record for most at-bats without a home run (1,354).

0 Missed starts by Don Sutton. The durable Dodgers right-hander never missed a start in 23 seasons.

0 World Series rings for Don Sutton with the Dodgers. They won the year before he arrived (1965) and the year after he left (1981).

0 Complete games by Roger Clemens in a Cy Young season. While with the Yankees in 2001, Clemens became the first starter without a complete game to win an American League Cy Young. Three years later, he also had no completions with Houston, then in the National League, to become the first Senior Circuit starter with that dubious distinction.

0 Perfect games by Armando Galarraga. On June 3, 2010, the Detroit right-hander pitched 8 2/3 perfect innings against Cleveland before umpire Jim Joyce called runner Jason Donald

VIDA BLUE

Image Credit: Ronnie Joyner

0 Pitchers who started All-Star Games in both leagues before Vida Blue. The left-handed pitcher became the first of five when he started for the National League in 1978 after opening for the American League seven years earlier. The four others who did it later were Max Scherzer, Roy Halladay, Randy Johnson, and Roger Clemens. Blue also won an MVP and Cy Young Award.

safe at first on a ground ball. Joyce later admitted he missed the call, which was never reversed.

0 Pitchers who started a season 20–1 before Roger Clemens.

0 Seasons with double-digits in no-hitters. There were a record nine no-hitters in 2021, plus two more that didn't count because they went just seven innings as part of a doubleheader.

0.25 Earned run average of Madison Bumgarner in five World Series starts, all with the San Francisco Giants. It accompanied his perfect 4–0 record.

0 Stephen Strasburg defeats during the first half of 2015. The Washington righty went 13–0.

0 Dallas Keuchel losses at home in 2015. He went 15–0 in 18 home starts for Houston.

0.75 Jake Arrieta's record-low earned run average from the 2015 All-Star Game to the end of the season.

0 Pitchers before 2017 with multiple home runs on Opening Day. Madison Bumgarner, then with the Giants, did it during the first game of the '17 season.

0 Runs allowed over 40 straight games by Ryan Pressly. The Houston reliever's record ended on May 24, 2019.

0 Mets with three straight Cy Youngs. Jacob deGrom had two in a row, winning his second in 2019, but none of Tom Seaver's three were consecutive.

0 No-hitters by Cy Young Award winners from the San Diego Padres. None of the team's four Cy Young pitchers ever hurled a no-hitter in Padres livery. In fact, the Friars got their first no-hitter from newcomer Joe Musgrove, a San Diego native, in 2021. Padres pitchers who won trophies without throwing no-hitters were Jake Peavy, Mark Davis, Randy Jones, and Gaylord Perry.

0 Regular season right-handed pitches thrown by Tommy John. The lefty famous for being the first successful recipient of elbow ligament reconstruction threw out the first pitch of the 1975 All-Star Game with his non-throwing hand. He missed all of 1975 and parts of 1974 and 1976 but came back strong, finishing with 288 wins, but said, "I'd rather be in Cooperstown than have a surgery named after me."

0 Active 300-game winners. Justin Verlander is closest but still quite far away.

0 Pitchers with 17 strikeout crowns. Nolan Ryan led his league a record 16 times.

0 Major-leaguers with 400 strikeouts in a season. Nolan Ryan fanned a record 383, one more than Sandy Koufax, but former big-leaguer Virgil Trucks holds the professional baseball record of 420 in 1938, his first pro season, in the Alabama-Florida League.

0 Active 300-game winners. Randy Johnson, the last man to win his 300th game, did so in 2009. Nobody else is even close to joining the 24 members of the 300-win club.

Image Credit: Ronnie Joyner

0 Number of Hall of Fame players in US Senate before Jim Bunning. The father of nine, who authored a 1964 Father's Day perfect game, was the only man elected to both the Baseball Hall of Fame and United States Senate. He represented Kentucky in both houses of Congress, serving from 1987 to 2011. Two baseball executives, Albert (Happy) Chandler of Kentucky and Morgan Bulkeley (Connecticut) previously served as senators and were also the only members of the Hall of Fame to serve as governors of their states.

0 Starts by Hall of Famer Bruce Sutter. He was the first Hall of Fame pitcher who served exclusively as a reliever.

0 Pitchers who yielded 3,000 walks. Nolan Ryan holds the record for walks allowed with 2,795.

0 Players who spent 28 years in the majors. Nolan Ryan holds the record with 27. The career strikeout king was also the only man to play for all four original expansion teams: the Mets, Astros, Rangers (nee Senators), and Angels.

0 Pitchers with immaculate innings in both leagues before Nolan Ryan. The Hall of Fame right-hander, who played for four different teams between 1966 and 1993, was the only pitcher to fan three batters on nine pitches in both leagues.

0 Pitchers who held hitters below the Mendoza Line in their careers. Hitters batted a record-low .204 against Nolan Ryan, who also holds the record for low-hit games (seven no-hitters, twelve one-hitters).

0 Pitchers with 20 low-hit games. The record is 19, by Nolan Ryan (seven no-hitters and 12 one-hitters). Ryan was 43 when he won his last strikeout crown and 44 when he pitched his last no-hitter. No man has ever done that at an older age.

0 Shutouts by David Cone after his perfect game. He was perfect for the Yankees on July 18, 1999, but never pitched a shutout again before retiring in 2003.

0 Twenty-win seasons for Mike Mussina before his last campaign. One of the most consistent starters in the majors, Mussina pitched for the Orioles and Yankees, winning 270 games and a berth in the Hall of Fame. But he never won 20 until his final year, when he went 20–9 while working 200 1/3 innings.

0 Twenty-win seasons for Dennis Martinez. The first major-leaguer from Nicaragua pitched a perfect game, was the first visiting pitcher to no-hit the Dodgers in Los Angeles, and won 245 games. But he never won 20 games in a season.

0 Wins by John Smoltz in 2002. Converted to closing after Tommy John elbow surgery, the Atlanta right-hander saved 55 games, a National League record, that year.

0 Pitchers before John Smoltz who reached Cooperstown after Tommy John surgery. The great Atlanta right-hander, elected in

2015, was the first pitcher to undergo the elbow ligament transplant and still make the Hall of Fame, though position player Paul Molitor, elected in 2004, also had the surgery.

0 Old-Timers' Days for Yankees pitcher. Roger Clemens, still active at age 44, was older than five of the players invited to 2007 Old-Timers' Day at Yankee Stadium. Four years earlier, he became the first pitcher to win his 300th game and strike out his 4,000th hitter in the same game.

0 Back-to-back homers yielded by Mariano Rivera in his first 850 games. The future Hall of Famer finally gave up consecutive home runs on May 7, 2009, after appearing 862 times. Carl Crawford and Evan Longoria of Tampa Bay connected in the ninth inning of an 8–6 win over the Yankees.

0 Number of years with three perfect games. It almost happened in 2009, when Dallas Braden pitched one on Mother's Day and Roy Halladay threw one weeks later, on May 29. Armando Galarraga missed joining them June 2 when umpire Jim Joyce blew a call at first base on the grounder that would have preserved the perfecto.

0 Father's Day no-hitters before World War II. Philadelphia's Jim Bunning, a father of nine, filled that void with a perfect game against the Mets at Shea Stadium in 1964. Not to be outdone, Dallas Braden of the Oakland A's later pitched a perfecto on Mother's Day.

0 No-hitters at Veterans Stadium before 1990. Journeyman Terry Mulholland of the Phillies had the first on August 15, 1990.

0.61 Earned run average of Dennis Eckersley in 1990, when he converted 48 of 50 save chances and more saves than base-runners allowed (41 hits and four walks in 73 1/3 innings). Two years later, he became the second closer to save 50 games in a season.

0 Walks in Clayton Kershaw's 2014 no-hitter. No previous no-hit pitcher has as many strikeouts (15) without giving up a walk. Only an error separated the Dodgers lefty from a perfect game.

0 National League pitchers with multiple no-hitters after turning 40. Nolan Ryan, who played a record 27 seasons, was the only man to throw more than one no-hitter while 40 or older. The Texas Rangers right-hander threw one at age 43 and another at 44, making him the oldest man to throw one.

0 No-hitters in four different countries in one year. The record is three, when Sean Manea threw one in Oakland, four Dodgers combined for another in Monterrey, and Canadian James Paxton pitched one in Toronto, all during the 2018 campaign.

0 Fifty-year-old pitchers to win in twentieth century. Jamie Moyer was 49 when he pitched the Rockies to a 5–3 win over Padres on April 17, 2012. He went seven innings.

0 Winning seasons for Warren Spahn as he aged. At age 43, the star southpaw suddenly went flat after his brilliant 1963 season, which included a 23–7 record and seven shutouts, and drifted from the Milwaukee Braves to the New York Mets and San Francisco Giants.

0 Runs allowed by Jamie Moyer in games during four different decades. A soft-tossing southpaw, Moyer was the only man to pitch shutouts in four decades—and the oldest man to pitch a shutout. He pitched 25 seasons, through 2012, and celebrated his 49th birthday in the big leagues.

0 Runs yielded by Jamie Moyer on May 7, 2010. That was the date the lefty became the oldest pitcher to throw a shutout, blanking the Atlanta Braves.

0 Bartolo Colon home runs over first 20 seasons. He finally connected at Petco Park on May 7, 2016, three weeks before his 43rd birthday, as the Mets beat the Padres, 6–3. No player hit his first home run at a more advanced age. P.S. Bartolo never hit another.

0 Latinos with more wins than Bartolo Colon. He had 247, topping Dennis Martinez and Juan Marichal.

0 Cy Young Award votes for Juan Marichal. He had six 20-win seasons en route to 243 wins but never won the award because he was in the same league as Sandy Koufax, Bob Gibson, and Tom Seaver.

0 Baseball gloves owned by Mariano Rivera when offered a tryout for professional baseball. He signed for $2,000, a pair of shoes, and a much-needed glove.

0 Official home runs for Mariano Rivera. The only unanimous Hall of Fame electee, Rivera had three official at-bats, four plate appearances, and one run batted in during his 19-year career. But he managed an inside-the-park home run at Yankee Stadium during 2019 Old-Timers' Day, five years after he retired.

0 Hall of Fame voters who omitted Mariano Rivera's name. The Yankees closer remains the only man elected to Cooperstown by unanimous vote. Derek Jeter fell one vote short of duplicating that feat.

0 World Series games won by the Washington Nationals in 2012. Concerned about an elbow, the team had shut down star pitcher Stephen Strasburg after 160 innings and failed to get past the NL Division Series without their hard-throwing young right-hander.

0 Throwback uniforms Chris Sale liked. He was suspended five games by his own team (then the Chicago White Sox) for cutting up replica old-time uniforms he didn't like.

Image Credit: Ronnie Joyner

0 Pitchers with 20 postseason wins. Andy Pettitte holds the record with 19 wins, against 11 defeats. All but one of those victories came while the lefty was pitching for the Yankees.

0 Blown saves by Zack Britton during relief streak. The lefty closer, then with the Baltimore Orioles, converted a record 55 in a row, an American League record, before it ended on July 23, 2017.

0 Staffs with four 200-strikeout pitchers before 2018. Cleveland became the first with Corey Kluber, Carlos Carrasco, Mike Clevenger, and Trevor Bauer.

0 Pitchers with 300 strikeouts in less than 200 innings during the twentieth century. The first man to do that was Gerrit Cole of the Houston Astros in 2019.

0 Pitchers before Gerrit Cole with 300 strikeouts but no complete games. Before Cole did it in 2019, when he fanned 316 of the 705 batters he faced while pitching for the Houston Astros, lefty Chris Sale was the most incomplete strikeout artist, going all the way just once when he fanned 308 hitters in 2017. In any of the 38 seasons with 300-strikeout pitchers, Cole threw the fewest innings (207 1/3). He also joined Houston teammate Justin Verlander in posting simultaneous 300-strikeout seasons, accomplished before only by Curt Schilling and Randy Johnson of the 2002 Arizona Diamondbacks.

0 Starters who averaged 11 strikeouts per nine innings. Randy Johnson, second to Nolan Ryan on the career strikeout list, holds the record with 10.61 Ks per nine.

0 Twentieth-century pitchers with five wins in a postseason. The first player to do that was Randy Johnson of the 2001 Arizona Diamondbacks.

0 No-hit authors before Justin Verlander to throw multiple hitless games in the same road venue. The Houston pitcher did it on September 1, 2019 when he threw a no-hitter at Toronto's Rogers Centre for the second time.

0 Pitchers before 2021 with double-digit strikeouts in a playoff game for three different teams. Max Scherzer, who had done it earlier for the Tigers and Nationals, did it for the Dodgers that year.

0 Pitchers on the wrong end of three no-hitters until 2021. Zack Plesac of Cleveland was the loser in three no-hit games—a dubious major-league mark.

0 Blown saves by Tyler Matzek in 2021. The Atlanta lefty set-up man had 24 holds, leading the National League in hold + save percentage, before becoming a postseason star.

0 Pitchers with 12 straight strikeouts. The record of 10 is shared by Tom Seaver, Aaron Nola, and Corbin Burnes.

0 Pitchers who started 17 openers. Hall of Famer Tom Seaver holds the record with 16, one more than Christy Mathewson.

0 Rookies of the Year who became 300-game winners—other than Tom Seaver. The award was created in 1947, in time for Jackie Robinson but not for Grover Cleveland Alexander, Christy Mathewson, or Walter Johnson.

0 Number of times Texas Rangers were no-hit at Globe Life Park, where they played 2,081 games. At Globe Life Field in 2021, however, they were victimized twice before Memorial Day.

0 Games won by Mets ace Jacob deGrom after the 2021 All-Star break. The former Cy Young Award winner was sidelined after July 7 with elbow issues and did not pitch again for more than a year.

0 Grand slams given up by Jacob deGrom in his career.

0 Grand slams allowed by Jim Palmer. The Hall of Fame right-hander was especially tough with the bases loaded.

0 Pitchers before 2021 whose first start was in a World Series game. Atlanta used rookie Dylan Lee in that role in Game 4 against the Astros. He only got one out in he first inning as Atlanta eventually eked out a 3–2 win.

0 Pitchers before Max Fried who fanned six without yielding a walk or run in a potential World Series clincher. The Atlanta lefty did that in Game 6 against the Houston Astros in 2021.

0 American League pitchers who hit 40 home runs in the twentieth century. Shohei Ohtani, a pitcher/DH for the Los Angeles Angels, hit 46 in 2021 en route to the American League's MVP award.

0 Home runs allowed by lethal lefty closer Josh Hader to left-handed hitters during the 2021 regular season. He yielded one—a fatal blow—in the NLDS, when Atlanta's Freddie Freeman hit a solo shot that proved the decisive marker in the fourth game.

0 Games pitched by Trevor Bauer in 2022. The former Cy Young Award winner was suspended two years by Major League Baseball after an investigation into alleged sexual violence.

0 Cy Young Awards for Gerrit Cole. Signed to a 10-year, $329 million contract by the Yankees after he hit free agency in 2019, Cole has come close to copping the pitching award but hasn't succeeded.

0 Runners allowed in the first six innings of consecutive Expansion Era games. Yankees teammates Jameson Taillon and Gerrit Cole threw at least six perfect innings in back-to-back games in June of 2022.

0 Runs allowed by Clay Holmes of the Yankees in 26 straight games. The former Pittsburgh farmhand proved flawless with a streak of 28 scoreless innings, longest for a Yankee since Mariano Rivera in 1999.

0 Games before 2022 in which twin brothers opposed each other. That changed after Taylor Rogers, a left-hander, was traded by the Twins to the Padres, who began the season against the Giants. Twin brother Tyler, a right-hander, is a submariner. They exchanged lineup cards before the game. They are the fifth set of twins to pitch in the same game but the first to pitch for rival teams. In their initial meeting, Taylor got the save and Tyler got the loss.

0 American League closers who worked 100 times in a season. Mike Marshall holds the record for appearances in both leagues: 106 in the National League and 90 in the American. In 1974, he worked a record 208 1/3 innings during those 106 outings—both relief records—and won the National League's Cy Young Award. Marshall's AL mark of 90 occurred in 1979. An offseason kinesiology professor at Michigan State, Marshall was a master of knowing how muscle tissues work, but his lifetime record was a pedestrian 97–112 with a 3.14 ERA and 188 saves.

0 Pitchers with eight Cy Young Awards. Roger Clemens had seven, fanned 20 men in nine-inning games 10 years apart, and collected his 300th win and 4,000 strikeout in the same game en route to 354 career victories.

0 Pitchers with 3,000 walks. Strikeout king Nolan Ryan holds the record with 2,795, less than half his total of 5,714 strikeouts.

0 Pitchers with 40-save seasons in both leagues before Jeff Reardon.

0 Defeats of Max Scherzer over 24 starts. The veteran right-hander went 15–0 with a 2.55 ERA between June 4, 2021 and May 8, 2022. In fact, his teams went 18–0 during those same starts. Scherzer, 37, began the '22 season with the New York Mets after splitting the previous season between the Washington Nationals and Los Angeles Dodgers.

0 Wins by Zack Greinke in the first two months of the 2022 season. An aging but talented right-hander signed by the Kansas City Royals, his former team, as a free agent, he went 0–3 with an unsightly 6.67 earned run average, six homers allowed, and a .335 opponents' average in six May starts.

0 Pitchers before Shohei Ohtani who homered the day after a double-digit strikeout game. Ohtani of the Angels fanned 10 and walked none on June 4, 2021, then homered the next day on the first pitch he saw in the first inning.

0 Players of the Live Ball Era with 10 homers and 10 wins in a season. Shohei Ohtani became the first in 2021.

0 Starting pitchers who batted twice before taking the mound. Two-way star Shohei Ohtani became the first to do that on April 20, 2022 when he batted twice for the Los Angeles Angels in the top of the first inning at Houston's Minute Maid Park. The Angels won, 6–0, with Ohtani fanning 12 in six innings of work.

Managers

0 World Series games played in 1904. Although the first World Series of the Modern Era was played in 1903, New York Giants manager John McGraw refused to play his AL counterparts a year later.

0 Pennants won by Ty Cobb as Tigers manager. He ran the team six years, finishing 35 games over .500, but never wound up in first place.

0 Ejections for Connie Mack. The longtime manager of the Philadelphia Athletics wore a business suit and did not swear—two reasons umpires never tossed him in a career that covered more than a half-century.

0 Pennants for the Washington Senators before 1924. That was the year the team tried "The Boy Wonder," 27-year-old Bucky Harris, as player-manager. He led the club to the 1924 world championship, hitting .333 with two home runs, and the 1925 AL pennant. Harris won another flag with the 1949 Yankees and became the fourth manager with 2,000 wins, managing until 1956.

0 Prewar managers to win flags with three teams. Bill McKechnie was the first, taking pennants with the 1925 Pirates, 1928 Cardinals, and 1939 and 1940 Reds.

0 First of five last words by George Stallings. "Oh, those bases on balls," the former manager said before he died in 1929.

0 Pilots with better winning percentage than Joe McCarthy. As manager of the Cubs and Yankees for 24 years, McCarthy won nine pennants and seven World Series while posting a record .614 winning percentage. His teams posted six 100-win seasons and never finished out of the first division.

0 Years Joe McCarthy played in majors. The Hall of Famer won pennants in both leagues and Ted Williams called him the best manager he ever had. But he never played in the big leagues.

0 Managers with 4,000 wins. Connie Mack tops the charts with 3,731, thanks to his 50-year tenure with the Philadelphia Athletics, but he also leads in losses with 3,948.

0 Managers who wore cap-and-gown at spring training after World War II. Casey Stengel, manager of the bottom-feeding Boston Braves, donned the garb when his team held spring training in Wallingford, Connecticut, near the prestigious Choate School for Boys, in 1943.

0 Full seasons Bucky Harris managed the Phillies. Hired in 1943, he lasted just 92 games before hands-on owner William Cox, later banned for gambling, dumped him with the team struggling.

0 Staying power of Mel Ott. On June 9, 1946, the mild-mannered manager of the New York Giants became the first pilot tossed from both games of a doubleheader. Pittsburgh won both.

0 Games managed by Leo Durocher in 1947. Suspended for a year by Commissioner Happy Chandler, the Brooklyn manager sat on the sidelines while Burt Shotton took over temporarily and helped Jackie Robinson through a tempestuous rookie season.

0 World Series wins for Al Lopez. In 15 years as a manager, his teams never had a losing record. Nor did they win a world championship, though he took the 1954 Indians and 1959 White Sox to the Fall Classic.

Image Credit: Ronnie Joyner

0 Years Yankees missed World Series with Billy Martin at second base. The team won AL flags in all of Martin's six years as a starter at the keystone between 1950 and 1956 but lost to Cleveland in 1954 when Martin was on military duty in the US Army. Martin returned from his military hitch in time to play the last 20 games of the 1955 season, another pennant year for the Yankees.

0 Multi-year contracts for Walter Alston. He managed the Dodgers, in Brooklyn and Los Angeles, for 23 seasons—all on one-year contracts. He won seven pennants, four World Series, and a record seven All-Star games en route to the Baseball Hall of Fame.

0 Games Solly Hemus managed against teams from New York. The only NL manager who never managed against a team based in New York, Hemus helmed the St. Louis Cardinals from 1959 to 1961, after the Dodgers and Giants left, before the Mets were created, and before the advent of interleague play.

0 Winning seasons for second-edition Senators not managed by Ted Williams. He was AL Manager of the Year in 1969 for his work with the team, but it was the only year the expansion team had a winning record.

0 Managers traded for each other before 1960, when Jimmy Dykes went from the Detroit Tigers to the Cleveland Indians for Joe Gordon in a midseason swap that was the first exchange of non-playing pilots.

0 Playoff losses for Miracle Mets. Under the steady hand of former first baseman Gil Hodges, the 1969 New York Mets—a perennial cellar-dweller since their founding as an expansion team seven years earlier—parlayed pitching and platooning into a potent unit that won the first NL East title and swept the favored Atlanta Braves in the first NL Championship Series. New York also knocked off the Baltimore Orioles in a five-game World Series. It was the only pennant won by Hodges, who died of a heart attack at age 47 while playing golf during 1972 spring training.

Image Credit: Ronnie Joyner

0 Gil Hodges went 0-for-34 in Baseball Hall of Fame elections before finally getting in via an era committee as part of the seven-man Class of 2022. Although he finished second to teammate Duke Snider in home runs and RBI during the '50s, Hodges was hurt by the fact that he never led the National League in a major offensive category (batting, home runs, runs batted in, or slugging percentage) or won an MVP award. A gifted defensive first baseman, he played for 18 years and managed for nine, taking the New York Mets to their first pennant and world championship in 1969.

0 Black managers before Frank Robinson. He was the first, as player-manager of the 1975 Cleveland Indians.

0 Managers before Sparky Anderson with world championships in both leagues. He won with the Cincinnati Reds and Detroit Tigers from 1970 to 1995, finishing with five pennants and three World Series wins. Tony La Russa later joined Anderson as managers who won world titles in both leagues.

0 Managers before Sparky Anderson to lose All-Star Games in both leagues. When the NL won, 6–1, for its 21st win in 23 games in 1985, the Detroit manager became the first pilot of losses for both leagues.

0 All-Star Game losses by Dick Williams, who managed teams from both leagues.

0 Montreal managers who won a pennant. Dick Williams came closest, finishing first during the 1981 split season. He won pennants with the Red Sox, Padres, and Athletics, winning the World Series twice (1972 and 1973) and a berth in the Baseball Hall of Fame (2007).

0 How hitters rated wiffle ball batting practice. Hall of Fame manager Dick Williams, then running the California Angels, held batting practice with wiffle balls in a hotel lobby during a team slump on the road. The hitters complained, but the actual hitting improved almost immediately.

0 Weeks Eddie Stanky managed the Rangers. Actually, his tenure lasted less than a day. Hired on June 23, 1977, he watched his new club lose, had a sleepless night, and decided he'd rather be home with his family.

0 Owners allowed to manage. Although Connie Mack owned and managed the Philadelphia Athletics for 50 years, the only other owner who tried to become field manager was Ted Turner of the 1977 Atlanta Braves. He lasted one day before Bowie Kuhn told him he couldn't do that.

0 Player-managers since Pete Rose. The career hit king held the dual role with the Reds from 1984 to 1986 but no one has done it since—anywhere in the majors.

0 Flags for Gene Mauch. The pilot of the Philadelphia Phillies had his team six-and-a-half games ahead with 12 to play in 1964 but squandered the lead and the pennant with a 10-game losing streak. The Phils finished tied with the Reds, both one game behind St. Louis. Mauch also managed the Twins and Angels, extending his frustrating managerial career to 26 years.

0 World Series titles in 4,272 games. Joe Torre appeared in that many games as player or manager before leading the Yankees to a world championship in 1996, his first year in the job. He later won three more World Series, including three straight from 1998 to 2000, and a berth in the Hall of Fame.

0 Years Joe Torre's Yankees missed the playoffs. He managed the team for 12 years (1996–2007), never failing to reach the postseason. A record for any manager hired by George Steinbrenner, he won nine division crowns, three wild-card spots, and two world championships.

Image Credit: Ronnie Joyner

0 Number of times Bobby Cox was ejected by Al Clark. All other umps combined to throw him out a record 158 times, plus three more in postseason play.

0 National League managers with seven 100-win seasons. Atlanta's Bobby Cox did it six times, the National League record.

0 Weeks Wally Backman managed in the majors. Hired by the Arizona Diamondbacks during the 2004 offseason, he lasted four days before the *New York Times* revealed that he had been arrested twice. He was fired and replaced by Bob Melvin.

0 Severe wiffle ball injuries before Rocco Baldelli. The one-time outfielder missed the entire 2005 season after tearing his left ACL while playing wiffle ball at his offseason Rhode Island home with his brother. He played five more years, then later became the youngest AL Manager of the Year at age 38 with the 2019 Minnesota Twins.

0 Games in pro ball for Mike Shildt. When he took over the St. Louis Cardinals in 2018, he became the first manager who had never played professional baseball.

0 Interviews cancelled by manager hit by a car. Mild-mannered Matt Williams, then manager of the Washington Nationals, hardly raised his voice when he was struck by a hit-and-run driver as a pedestrian while calling into a radio show.

0 Years of managerial experience Aaron Boone had before becoming Yankees manager. The former major-league third baseman stepped right from the ESPN *Sunday Night Baseball* booth into the Yankees dugout.

0 New Mets managers to win their first three games before Buck Showalter. He became the first in 2022.

0 World championships for Dusty Baker as manager before 2022. He took five different teams to the playoffs but never won the final round.

Executives & Enforcers

Executives

0 High school diplomas for Kenesaw Mountain Landis. The first Commissioner of Baseball was a high school dropout who later decided to study law.

0 Women who owned a team before Helene Britton. At age 32, she became president of the St. Louis Cardinals through inheritance shortly after the turn of the twentieth century. An early women's rights advocate, she attended all National League meetings and sought to increase female attendance at games by hiring a handsome male singer to perform between innings.

0 Days that passed between the end of the Black Sox trial and their ouster from baseball. Eight players accused of involvement in a scheme to fix the 1919 World Series so that the Chicago White Sox lost to the underdog Cincinnati Reds were banned from the game by Kenesaw Mountain Landis.

0 World championships for Tom Yawkey. He bought the Boston Red Sox in 1933 and spent the next 44 years building the ballclub, taking American League pennants in 1946, 1967, and 1975, but never won the World Series.

0 Night games before 1935. Innovative executive Larry MacPhail not only was the first to light a big-league park but followed the Crosley Field debut by adding lights to Ebbets Field and Yankee Stadium as he changed jobs. Intended as a novelty limited to seven games per season, night baseball was so well received that every team added lights—with the Chicago Cubs completing the process on 8/8/88 (officially 8/9/88 because of rain on the earlier date).

0 World Series games watched by Phil Wrigley while he was answering fan mail. The owner of the Cubs, responding to complaints from irate fans who couldn't get tickets for the Cubs-Tigers matchup in 1945, missed the first three World Series games as a result.

0 Sunday games for Branch Rickey. As a player, manager, and executive, Branch Rickey refused to sacrifice his religious beliefs for the game. He was never at the ballpark on Sunday and used Burt Shotton, among others, as his "Sunday manager" for both St. Louis teams.

0 Games played by the Continental League. Branch Rickey's proposed third major league collapsed when the existing majors expanded into several of his cities starting in 1961.

0 Attendance for Bill Veeck speech in St. Louis. Midwinter dates for back-to-back promotion appearances for the St. Louis Browns owner didn't go according to plan. After speaking at a dinner in Springfield, Illinois, Veeck drove directly to St. Louis for a noontime luncheon. But a driving blizzard forced him to park and walk when he was 90 minutes away. On crutches because he lost a leg during World War II, Veeck didn't have a hat or coat but did have the determination to keep his date. He arrived exactly at noon to find no one else had ventured out in the storm.

0 Teams wearing shorts. Bill Veeck's 1976 experiment didn't last. Long known as "the P.T. Barnum of Baseball," Veeck believed he could bring fans through the turnstiles by offering endless promotions. One of them was outfitting his Chicago White Sox in shorts during the '76 season. The players complained—and got sliding burns—and the idea was "short"-lived.

0 Times Buck O'Neil batted in the majors, having been blocked from the big leagues by segregation. But the erstwhile first baseman of the Kansas City Monarchs became the first black coach, with the 1962 Chicago Cubs; an ambassador for baseball; and eventually a posthumous electee to the Baseball Hall of Fame.

0 Father-and-son tandems in Cooperstown. Although there were numerous fathers and sons who played major-league baseball, none were selected separately. But the 1988 selection of Lee MacPhail, son of previously-enshrined executive Larry MacPhail, gave the institution its first paternal pair.

0 Reversals of lifetime suspension received by Pete Rose. After the career hits king was banned for life by Bart Giamatti for allegedly betting on baseball, he made several appeals for reinstatement, none successfully.

0 Months lived by Bart Giamatti after he banned Pete Rose. Eight days after banning the career hits leader for gambling on August 24, 1989, Commissioner Giamatti died.

0 Members of Montreal Expos Hall of Fame before Charles Bronfman. The expansion team's first owner was also the first man elected to the team's Hall of Fame. He was also the first to have a number retired in his honor. No. 83, selected to match his age, was placed on the right-field wall of Olympic Stadium.

0 Apologies issued by Marge Schott. The outspoken Reds owner was banned for life by Bud Selig in 1996, but reinstated "for good behavior" in 1998.

0 Tolerance for bigoted owners in Major League Baseball. Marge Schott, owner of the Cincinnati Reds, was suspended in 1999 after praising Adolf Hitler and condemning Eric Davis, one of her own players, with racial slurs. She was eventually pressured into selling her team.

0 Owners suspended since George Steinbrenner. Given a two-year suspension by Bowie Kuhn in 1974 for making illegal campaign contributions, he drew another lifetime ban from Fay Vincent in 1990 for paying Howard Spira $40,000 to gather dirt on star outfielder Dave Winfield. Three years later, Bud Selig lifted the ban and Steinbrenner celebrated by dressing like Napoleon and mounting a white horse for a *Sports Illustrated* cover.

0 Executives before 1995 with world titles in both leagues. When John Schuerholz won the World Series with the 1985 Kansas City Royals and 1995 Atlanta Braves, he became the first general manager to do that. His Braves also won 14 straight division titles, a major-league record. He was elected to the Hall of Fame in 2017.

0 Twentieth-century college roommates who became big-league general managers. That changed in the twenty-first century, when former Cornell University roommates Jon Daniels and A. J. Preller became general managers of the Texas Rangers and San Diego Padres, respectively. Preller had worked for Daniels in Texas, where he was assistant general manager, before San Diego hired him.

0 Women elected to Cooperstown in the twentieth century. The first was Effa Manley, the late owner of the Newark Eagles, a Negro Leagues team. When elected in 2006, she became the first female member of the Baseball Hall of Fame.

0 Players losing multi-homer games to videotape replay before Josh Donaldson. On September 8, 2015, he lost two home runs in one game when instant replay revealed balls he hit were foul.

0 Numbers of times owners and players met during the first 42 days of 2021 lockout. The work stoppage lasted 99 days, cut several weeks off spring training, and forced rescheduling of the regular season's opening week.

Enforcers

0 Tolerance by umpire Bill Klem. One day after Brooklyn catcher Al Lopez complained that Klem blew a call at the plate, Lopez taped a newspaper photo to the plate, covered it with dirt, and waited. Predictably, Klem cleaned the plate—and threw Lopez out of the game.

0 Early umpires who used arm signals. Bill Klem, an umpire from 1905 to 1941, was reputed to be the first. He was deployed almost exclusively behind the plate because of his ability to call balls and strikes.

0 Umpires who worked 20 World Series. Bill Klem holds the record with 18. He umped for 37 years, also a major-league mark.

0 Umpires who ejected 35 men in a season. The record is 33 by Mal Eason in 1914. He even had six in one day on June 29 of that year.

0 Players ejected by umpire Tom Connolly for 10 straight seasons. An umpire for 35 years early in the twentieth century, he was a British import known for his dignity and composure. He was in the umpiring crew of the first World Series in 1903 and was elected to the Hall of Fame in 1953.

0 Early players who jumped from the bench to the blue. Jocko Conlan was the first, as a backup Chicago White Sox outfielder asked to fill in as an umpire in 1935. He was so good at it that he umpired in five World Series and was elected to the Hall of Fame in 1974.

0 Innings missed in 16 years by an umpire. Bill McGowan umped for 2,541 consecutive games, a streak that made him the umpiring equivalent of Cal Ripken Jr. He reached the Hall of Fame in 1992.

0 Six-umpire crews working World Series games before World War II. The first six-man team worked the 1947 World Series between the Dodgers and Yankees.

Image Credit: Ronnie Joyner

0 Umpires with their names on their hats before Al Clark. When American League umpires added the initials "AL" to their caps in 1975, the timing couldn't have been better for Al Clark, who reached the majors a year later. The New Jersey native also was the first arbiter to wear glasses on a regular basis and the first Jewish umpire hired by the AL. League umpiring staffs merged in 2000.

0 Players in both baseball and football Halls of Fame. But Cal Hubbard, a football lineman and baseball umpire, is the only man in both.

0 Three-generational umpires before the Runge family. Grandfather Ed Runge, father Paul, and son Brian were the first in baseball history.

0 Umpires who wore the outside chest protector after 1985. That's when Jerry Neudecker, the last man to use the balloon protector, retired.

0 Regular umpires who started the 1995 season. For the second time, Major League Baseball required replacement umpires in order to start a season. Labor negotiations with the umpires union were soon settled.

0 Progress made by umpires and MLB before Richard Nixon became federal mediator. With labor talks stalled in 1985, the two sides agreed on binding arbitration to settle the impasse. They also agreed on the former president when the umpires union suggested him to mediate. Instead of granting the umpires' request for $1,000 more per man when the playoffs expanded, Nixon granted $10,000 per man. The Players Association had already secured an increase for the extra games when the LCS expanded from best-of-five to best-of-seven.

0 Times Gaylord Perry was ejected in first 20 seasons. The streak ended on August 23, 1982, when home-plate umpire Dave Phillips threw the suspected spitball pitcher out in the seventh inning of a game against Boston. Phillips, who had warned

Perry previously about doctoring the ball, reacted after Seattle catcher Jim Essian threw the ball back to Perry after the ump sought to inspect it.

0 Umpires with 5,000 appearances before 2006. Bruce Froemming was the first to do that.

0 Reliance on instant replay before 2008. Introduced on August 28, 2008, videotape replay quickly cost Alex Rodriguez a home run but gave one to Carlos Peña. When used in the World Series for the first time a year later, A-Rod was the first beneficiary: his foul became a home run.

0 Orange baseballs used in the majors. Charlie Finley, mercurial and enigmatic owner of the Oakland Athletics, tried them in exhibition games only.

0 Initial support for North Side ballpark. The Chicago Planning Commission rejected plans for the future Wrigley Field in 1908 because members thought it would snarl horse and buggy traffic.

0 Warning tracks at Crosley Field. Like many prewar ballparks, the home of the Cincinnati Reds from 1912 to 1970 did not have a warning track. Instead, it had an incline called "the Terrace" that warned outfielders they were nearing the wall.

0 American League clubs in Federal League ballparks. The last remnant of the upstart Federal League, which lasted only two seasons, is Wrigley Field, home of the Chicago Cubs, a National League team. The stadium, first called Weeghman Park, opened in 1914.

0 Braves Field homers over the left-field barrier in the park's first decade. The cavernous Boston ballpark, biggest in the majors when it opened in 1915, not only held 40,000 fans but had a streetcar line that ran right into the ballpark. Nobody homered over its left-field fence in the first 11 years Braves Field was open, but four New York Giants hit inside-the-park homers in the same game on April 29, 1922.

0 Cost overruns on the original Yankee Stadium. The Bronx ballpark, immediately dubbed "The House That Ruth Built" upon opening in 1923 because of Babe Ruth's drawing power, cost $2.4 million ($345M in 2000 dollars).

0 Yankee Stadium monuments in fair territory. That was not always the case, as the original three monuments—honoring Babe Ruth, Lou Gehrig, and the late manager Miller Huggins—were in fair territory in deep center field, along with the flagpole. The park now has six monuments, 23 retired numbers, and 40 plaques honoring former players, managers, executives, broadcasters, and even two popes who visited Yankee Stadium.

0 Teams with public address systems before 1929. The New York Giants became the first on August 25 of that year in a game against the Pittsburgh Pirates.

0 Sunday games in Fenway before 1932. Even after Boston's ban on Sunday ball was lifted in 1929, the Red Sox couldn't play at home because Fenway Park stood less than 1,000 feet from a church. Thinking ahead, the team got permission to play 13 Sunday games and three holiday dates at nearby Braves Field. A Sunday curfew law still curtailed double-header nightcaps until it was finally lifted in the '50s.

0 Balls hit over the Briggs Stadium right-field seats before 1939. Red Sox rookie Ted Williams cleared the barrier in his first at-bat in Detroit on May 4 of that year.

0 Prewar ballparks with organists. Wrigley Field, home of the Chicago Cubs, became the first in 1941, two years after the Second World War started.

0 Black fans allowed in St. Louis grandstand before World War II. The last city to integrate its seating areas, St. Louis barred black fans from buying grandstand tickets until May 4, 1944. They had been restricted to the bleachers.

0 Night games in 1943. They were banned because of wartime blackout restrictions.

0 Spring training games in Arizona until 1947. Before the advent of air-conditioning, Arizona was widely considered too unpleasant for spring training. But that changed in 1947, when the Cleveland Indians and New York Giants pitched camp there.

0 Games in Panama for 67 years. Between 1947 spring training and a Yankees-Marlins exhibition series designed to salute Panamanian pitcher Mariano Rivera of the Yankees in 2014, no games were played in Panama.

0 Pennants for Pittsburgh with Hank Greenberg. After obtaining American League slugger Hank Greenberg in 1947, the Pirates reduced the distance from home plate to left field by 30 feet and to left-center by 20 feet. The new section, quickly dubbed "Greenberg Gardens," was changed to "Kiner's Korner" for Ralph Kiner when Greenberg retired after one NL season. But the Pirates didn't win a pennant until 1960, after both were long retired.

0 Advertising billboards allowed at Forbes Field. With the sole exception of a wartime recruiting sign for the Marines, there were no ads posted during the 61 years the Pittsburgh Pirates played there.

0 Spring training games in Florida during most of World War II. Teams were told to find facilities close to home so that the nation's railroads could serve military needs first.

0 Years Brooklyn Dodgers drew 2 million fans to Ebbets Field. Their single-season peak in Brooklyn was 1,807,526 in 1947. The day after Sal Maglie threw a no-hitter in 1956, the crowd at Ebbets for the Braves-Dodgers game was 7,847.

0 National League All-Star wins at Ebbets Field. Only one game was played in the Brooklyn ballpark, in 1949, and the American League won it, 11–7. But the game was noteworthy for the initial inclusion of black players: Jackie Robinson, Roy Campanella, Don Newcombe, and Larry Doby.

0 Number of times Mel Ott fanned 70 times in a season. The New York Giants slugger made good contact, never striking out more than 69 times while hitting 511 home runs, 325 of them aided by the short right-field porch of the Polo Grounds. His 10th-inning homer won Game 7 of the 1933 World Series against Washington.

0 Dodgers who won two suits in one game from Abe Stark sign. The Ebbets Field advertising sign, put up before World War II by the Brooklyn clothier, said HIT SIGN, WIN SUIT. But the only man to do it twice in a game was Woody English of the Chicago Cubs.

0 Dodger Stadium games before 1962. The Los Angeles Dodgers spent their first four years in the Los Angeles Coliseum, a cavernous facility best suited for football, after leaving Brooklyn's Ebbets Field.

0 Yankee Stadium wins for Chicago Cubs. Apparently spooked by The House That Ruth Built and its successors in the Bronx, the Cubs lost all 12 of their games there, including interleague games and sweeps in the 1932 and 1938 World Series.

0 Aquariums in the majors outside of Tampa Bay. Cownose stingrays common to the waters of Tampa Bay live in a ten-thousand-gallon-gallon inside-the-ballpark tank at Tropicana Field, home of the Tampa Bay Rays in St. Petersburg, Florida. Cared for by staffers from the Florida Aquarium, the enormous creatures also have plenty of company from fans during games.

0 American League rotundas outside of Tropicana Park. The home of the Tampa Bay Rays, opened in 1990, has a rotunda similar to the one Ebbets Field used to have.

0 Mile-high seats before Coors Field. A row of seats in the upper deck of the Denver ballpark is painted purple to designate an altitude of 5,280 feet above sea level—one mile high. No wonder the home team is called the Colorado Rockies.

0 Baseball games in Washington between transfer of Senators and arrival of Nationals. The nation's capital was without a team for 33 years between 1972, when the second-edition Senators became the Texas Rangers, and 2005, when the Expos morphed into the Washington Nationals.

0 Twentieth-century games in San Juan. The first official game in the Puerto Rico capital was the 2001 season opener between the Jays and Rangers, played on April 1, though the Montreal Expos played 43 "home" games there in 2003 and 2004 before relocating to Washington as the Nationals.

0 Retro ballparks before Camden Yards. The home of the Baltimore Orioles, opened in 1992, was a new park with a retro look that was copied by many other clubs. It featured an old brick Baltimore & Ohio Railroad warehouse, built in 1905.

0 Cars on Roberto Clemente Bridge. Open only to pedestrians during Pirates home games, the gold-colored overpass over the Allegheny River is visible from PNC Park, one of the most photogenic in the majors. It was named for the legendary Pittsburgh slugger, who lost his life in a plane crash while trying to ferry earthquake relief to Nicaragua.

0 Bigger fountains than the one at Kauffman Stadium. When it opened in the early '70s, the stadium featured a water display that was the largest privately-funded fountain on the planet. It measured 322 feet wide.

0 Third edition of the Washington Senators. The San Diego Padres were set to become the third incarnation of the Washington Senators early in 1974 but stayed put after an 11th-hour offer to buy the team by McDonald's founder Ray Kroc. The original Senators moved to Minneapolis-St. Paul in 1961 and were replaced by an expansion franchise. When that team left to become the Texas Rangers in 1972, the capital had no ballclub until the Montreal Expos moved there in 2005 and became the Washington Nationals.

0 National League teams before 2006 that won a world championship in the first year of a new ballpark. The St. Louis Cardinals stopped that streak when they opened the new Busch Stadium and went all the way to a World Series title.

0 Cool pools in hot climates. That changed in 1998 with the opening of the domed downtown ballpark in Phoenix. Chase Field, home of the National League's Arizona Diamondbacks since 1998, has an 8,500-gallon tank just behind the right-field fence.

0 Ball hunters in boats outside of San Francisco. When the San Francisco Giants have home games at Oracle Park, located on the waterfront, a raft of kayaks, boats, and small vessels waits for home run balls to clear the right-field fence and land in San Francisco Bay. It is named for Hall of Famer Willie McCovey, a left-handed slugger who often hit long balls to right field.

0 Green Monster seats before 2003. That was the year the Red Sox installed seating atop the 37-foot-high wall in left field at Fenway Park.

0 Chance Colorado can break its own attendance record. Playing in Mile High Stadium, a converted football park, the team drew a record 4.5 million fans in 1993, its first season. But the new Coors Field, which opened two years later, had a much smaller capacity (50,480).

0 Lights at McKechnie Field in Bradenton, Florida, before 2008. The oldest spring training ballpark, built in 1923, was the last to add lights for night play.

0 Dugouts at Holman Field, the Vero Beach, Florida, facility that served as spring training home of the Dodgers for 60 years.

0 Attendance for a 2015 Oriole Park game. The public was barred in the wake of widespread unrest following the death of Freddie Gray while in policy custody. Baltimore beat the Chicago White Sox, 8–2.

0 Enclosed press boxes for London Series. Broadcasters worked from the open stands during the initial London Series, a two-game set between the Boston Red Sox and New York Yankees on June 28-29, 2019.

0 Attendance during the first year of the COVID-19 pandemic. With fans barred from ballparks during the virus-shortened 2020 season, teams used cardboard cutouts and canned crowd cheers to offset the emptiness caused by the absence of customers.

0 Major-league parks named after star players. Most have corporate names, though some are named after owners (Turner Field, Wrigley Field) or have team names (Dodger Stadium, Yankee Stadium, Nationals Park). The Braves were pressured to name their new suburban park after the legendary Hank Aaron but decided instead to sell their name-changing rights to Sun Trust Bank. The stadium is now called Truist Park. Comiskey Park,

Griffith Stadium, and Connie Mack Stadium were named after owners who started as players but were elected to the Hall of Fame as executives.

0 Perfect games at CitiField. The home of the Mets, opened in 2009, has never been the scene of a perfect game.

0 Years Wrigley Field and Fenway Park were in same World Series. The game's two most historic parks, now more than a century old, were never in the World Series at the same time—mainly because both the Cubs and Red Sox suffered long championship droughts.

0 Homers in every game of a four-game series by a Cubs player at Wrigley Field. Joey Votto of the visiting Reds did it in 2021, but such legendary Chicago sluggers as Ernie Banks, Billy Williams, Ron Santo, and Hank Sauer never did.

0 Players before 2022 with Nationals Park homers five games in a row. Atlanta shortstop Dansby Swanson became the first to connect five games in a row at the Washington ballpark on June 15, 2022.

0 Official games overseas in the twentieth century. That changed in the year 2000, when the Chicago Cubs and New York Mets started the season in Japan's Tokyo Dome.

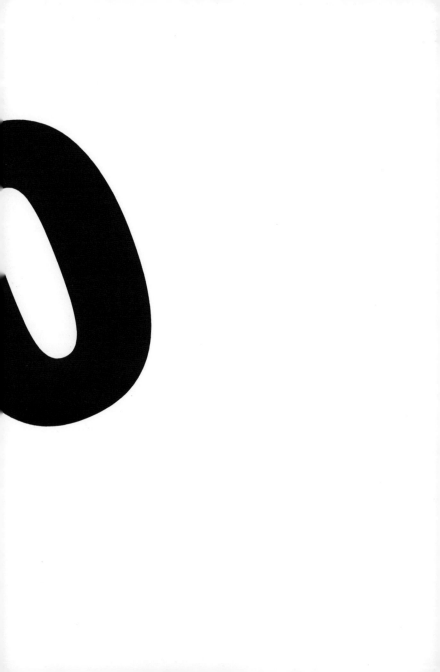

Trades

O Days Babe Ruth played for Connie Mack. The owner-manager of the Philadelphia Athletics passed on a chance to purchase the future home run king from the minor-league Baltimore Orioles, an independent team, in 1914. Instead, the O's sold Ruth, Ernie Shore, and Ben Egan to the Boston Red Sox for the total price of $25,000.

O Satisfaction for Rogers Hornsby in St. Louis. After winning six straight National League batting crowns and leading the Cardinals to their first world championship in his first year as player-manager, Hornsby wanted a reward: a three-year, $150,000 contract. Though Hornsby was popular in St. Louis, the Cards traded him to the New York Giants for fellow second baseman Frankie Frisch and Jim Ring. The deal still ranks as one of the biggest blockbusters in baseball history.

O Pennants won by Red Sox after Lefty Grove arrived. After helping Connie Mack's Philadelphia A's win consecutive World Series in 1929-30-31, Lefty Grove left for Boston in a cost-cutting, five-player, Depression-era deal on December 12, 1933. Grove stayed eight years, never posting a losing record, but never winning another pennant either. He finished with 300 wins.

O Commute involved when Ralph Kiner was traded. The slugging Pittsburgh outfielder, later a popular broadcaster, was the center of a 10-man trade on June 4, 1953. Word of the deal between the Pirates and Cubs broke before the two teams were to play at Forbes Field, so Kiner and the others involved merely had to switch clubhouses. Nancy Kiner, arriving late that day, said she couldn't understand why her husband was wearing a different uniform.

0 St. Louis Browns teammates who outlasted Don Larsen. The last man to retire from the defunct St. Louis Browns, Larsen was better remembered as the author of the only perfect game in World Series history. He did it in 1956, two years after the Yankees acquired him from Baltimore in a 17-man trade, the largest in baseball history.

0 Trades involving Stan Musial, who spent all 22 of his big-league summers in St. Louis. Both tiny Hack Wilson (above) and towering Hank Greenberg (below) were sluggers of the '30s who starred for several clubs.

0 All-Star selections for Ernie Broglio. Just 28 when swapped from the Cardinals to the Cubs for Lou Brock in a six-man swap on June 15, 1964, the former 20-game winner fizzled immediately. Never an All-Star, he went 7–19 in three seasons on the North Side and is remembered only as the man traded for the best basestealer in the history of the National League.

0 National League Triple Crowns for Frank Robinson. Four years after winning the National League's MVP award with the pennant-winning Reds of 1961, Frank Robinson found himself traded across league lines to the Baltimore Orioles. The 30-year-old slugger responded by winning the 1966 American League Triple Crown—something he had never done in the NL—and the MVP award, thus becoming the first (and so far only player) to win the trophy in both leagues. The Orioles won four pennants and a world championship during Robinson's six-year tenure.

0 Days Dick Allen played for Atlanta. Refusing a 1974 deal from the Chicago White Sox because he didn't want to play in the Deep South, the former American League MVP was dealt back to his original team: the Philadelphia Phillies.

0 Games Rollie Fingers and Joe Rudi played for the Red Sox. Sold to Boston by Oakland owner Charlie Finley in 1976 before they could leave as free agents, the two stars actually suited up in Red Sox uniforms but never got into a game. Commissioner Bowie Kuhn vetoed the sales as violating "the best interests of baseball" and returned both players to the A's. They left on their own after the season ended.

0 Games Jeff Bagwell played for Boston. Born in Boston and raised in Connecticut, he dreamed of playing in Fenway Park but

instead was swapped across league lines to the Houston Astros on August 31, 1990—in an even-up swap for aging reliever Larry Andersen. Moving from third to first a year later, Bagwell became a Hall of Famer who spent his entire career in Houston.

0 Home runs by Nick Esasky in Atlanta. After hitting 30 for the Boston Red Sox in 1989, the first baseman signed with the Braves but developed vertigo in spring training and played only nine games, never hitting a home run or knocking in a run, before a premature retirement.

0 Flags for expansion teams. Newly-created clubs usually languish near the bottom of the standings for years. But the 1999 Arizona Diamondbacks succeeded almost instantly, parlaying trades and free-agent signings into a juggernaut that jumped from 97 losses the year before to 100 wins—good for a comfortable 14-game margin of victory in the NL West. The team not only led the National League in runs scored but also produced potent pitching as towering left-hander Randy Johnson, the most prominent signee, won the first of four straight Cy Young Awards.

0 Interest in adding payroll. The Miami Marlins have made multiple transactions designed to reduce payroll. They unloaded future Triple Crown winner Miguel Cabrera, sending him to Detroit in an eight-man deal after the 2007 season; moved Mark Buehrle and four other veterans to Toronto in a twelve-man trade five years later; and sent Giancarlo Stanton to the Yankees in a four-man deal before the end of 2017. Stanton had just led the majors with 59 home runs and 132 runs batted in.

0 Longevity for four Brewers prospects dealt to the Marlins for Christian Yelich. While the slugging outfielder went on to win

an MVP award, none of the four men traded for him—Lewis Brinson, Jordan Yamamoto, Monte Harrison, or Isan Diaz—did anything much for the Marlins.

0 Games won by Cole Hamels and Felix Hernandez in Atlanta. Seeking veteran pitchers to balance a young staff, the 2020 Braves signed both but then lost Hamels to a series of injuries and Hernandez to COVID-19, which caused him to opt out of his contract for health reasons. Hamels wound up giving the Braves a total of three innings—three more than King Felix.

0 Games played by the Panda in Cleveland. Acquired from Atlanta for Eddie Rosario at the 2021 trading deadline, Pablo Sandoval drew his immediate release from the Indians and never played again. Rosario, on the other hand, went on to be MVP of the NL Championship Series against the Dodgers.

0 Reasons for the Red Sox to keep Mookie Betts. After Boston won the 2018 World Series, thanks in part to Betts, the team dropped to third place, a distant 19 games behind, in 2019 and decided to pare payroll and rebuild for the future. The biggest move was sending Betts, then 27, and his hefty contract to the Los Angeles Dodgers, along with high-priced pitcher David Price and $48 million, for Alex Verdugo and two other prospects before 2020 spring training. As a result, the Red Sox finished last and Dodgers became world champions for the first time since 1988. Betts, a former American League MVP, could have become a free agent after the '21 season but signed a long-term extension with Los Angeles. He also became a strong candidate to join Frank Robinson as the only men to win MVP trophies in both leagues.

0 Passed balls by Jacob Stallings in 2021. The Gold Glove catcher, then with the Pittsburgh Pirates, was subsequently traded to the Miami Marlins.

0 Calls Freddie Freeman got from the Braves with free agency approaching. The first baseman, who had spent his entire 12-year tenure in Atlanta, said he wanted to stay there but never got an offer to extend his contract. After the Braves obtained Matt Olson from Oakland in March 2022, the former National League MVP signed a six-year, $162 million pact with the Los Angeles Dodgers.

0 Home runs by slugger Marcus Semien in first month with Texas. The high-priced free agent infielder, who hit 45 home runs for Toronto in 2021, failed to hit one in his first 158 plate appearances for the Rangers in 2022.

0 Tolerance for Trevor Bauer. The former National League Cy Young Award winner drew a two-year suspension in 2022 for violating Major League rules against domestic violence after several women complained. Three years earlier, he was fined and traded on the same day (July 28) after throwing the ball over the outfield wall during removal from the game by Cleveland manager Terry Francona. The team then included him in a three-way swap that also involved the Cincinnati Reds, who got Bauer, and the San Diego Padres.

0 Dollars for Correa before Donaldson deal. Only after the Minnesota Twins moved Josh Donaldson to the New York Yankees in a mid-March trade did the team find the dollars to sign prized shortstop Carlos Correa for the 2022 season. The former Houston standout got a three-year pact with an annual base of $35.1 million, the largest ever given an infielder.

Games

World Series

0 World Series that went nine games. Although four Fall Classics were played with a best-of-nine format, none ever went the distance.

0 World championships for the Boston Braves after 1914. The team finished first in 1948 too but failed to beat the Cleveland Indians in the World Series. Then it moved to Milwaukee in 1953 and Atlanta in 1966. The 1914 team was the first to reach postseason play after falling 16 games under .500 during the season. They were 26–40 and 15 games behind the New York Giants after losing a July 4 doubleheader but caught fire, going 67–19 for a blistering .779 winning percentage afterward. The "Miracle Braves" won the pennant by 10 1/2 games and the World Series in four straight over the favored Philadelphia Athletics.

0 World Series games for Kiki Cuyler in 1927. Although the 26-year-old outfielder was the hero of the 1925 Pittsburgh world championship team, manager Donie Bush—nursing a grudge— benched him against the Yankees in 1927, allowing New York to sweep. A .321 career hitter who eventually reached Cooperstown, Cuyler was traded to the Cubs after the 1927 campaign.

0 Players ejected during the first 20 years of the World Series. The first man thrown out was Heinie Manush in 1933.

0 Pinch-homers in the World Series before the Second World War. Yogi Berra delivered the first, connecting for the Yankees against the Brooklyn Dodgers in 1947.

0 Home runs in first World Series at-bat by 500-home run club members before Mel Ott. The lefty slugger of the New York Giants was the first man to do that.

0 Runs scored by the Yankees in two tries against Lew Burdette in 1957 World Series. The fidgety right-hander threw three complete games, two of them shutouts, as the Milwaukee Braves beat the favored Yankees in seven games. Burdette thus matched the entire American League, which managed just two shutouts against the Yankees that season.

0 World Series night games before 1971. That was the year the Pirates and Orioles played the first and started a trend that quickly became universal.

0 Road wins in World Series by 2017 Astros. The team won all four games at Minute Maid Park, helped in part by an elaborate sign-stealing system that cost the jobs of manager A. J. Hinch and general manager Jeff Luhnow when discovered by Major League Baseball.

0 Extra-base hits by Willie Mays in 1951 World Series. After leading the New York Giants to the NL pennant, the rookie out-fielder fell apart against the Yankees in the Fall Classic. He hit .182 with no extra-base hits as the Giants lost in six games.

0 Yankees-Dodgers World Series games missed by Pee Wee Reese. The Dodgers shortstop was the only man to play in all 44 meetings of the arch-rivals from 1941 to 1956.

0 Players who hit safely in 18 straight World Series games. Hank Bauer, an outfielder with the Yankees who later managed the Orioles to a World Championship, holds the record at 17.

0 Runs scored by Pittsburgh Pirates in two games of 1960 World Series. The Bucs lost games by scores of 16–3, 10–0, and 12–0 and were outscored by the Yankees, 55–27, but won in seven games. The decisive blow was Bill Mazeroski's Game 7 ninth-inning leadoff homer—the first one to end a World Series.

0 World Series homers for Ted Williams. Although he batted .344 with 521 home runs during a career interrupted twice by wartime military service, the Red Sox slugger hardly hit in the 1946 World Series, which Boston lost to the St. Louis Cardinals.

Image Credit: Ronnie Joyner

0 World Series MVPs from losing teams before 1960. Bobby Richardson of the losing Yankees won the award that year after collecting a record 12 runs batted in during the seven-game set.

0 Years before 1976 that a team swept the playoffs and World Series. Then Cincinnati's Big Red Machine swept the NL Championship Series, a best-of-five, from the Philadelphia Phillies and the best-of-seven World Series from the New York Yankees.

0 World titles for Royals before 1985. The first team to overcome 3–1 deficits in games twice in the same postseason, the Kansas City Royals won their first world championship by beating the St. Louis Cardinals. The Royals won another crown in 2015, defeating the New York Mets.

Image Credit: Ronnie Joyner

0 Pitchers before Roy Face with three saves in a World Series. The star closer of the Pittsburgh Pirates became the first in 1960, when he saved three games against the Yankees in a seven-game Fall Classic. The only Pittsburgh win he didn't save came in the decisive Game 7, a 10-9 win ended by Bill Mazeroski's leadoff homer in the bottom of the ninth at Forbes Field.

0 World Series games for Vince Coleman in 1985. The fleet St. Louis outfielder, on the field before Game 4 of the NL Championship Series against the Dodgers, did not realize the automatic tarpaulin, which weighed half a ton, was sneaking up on him. It caught his legs, knocking him out of the playoffs and World Series that followed. Minus their sparkplug, the Cards lost to the Royals in seven games.

0 Runs scored by Lonnie Smith in last game of 1991 World Series. He was on first with nobody out in the top of the eighth but failed to score when Terry Pendleton doubled because he was decoyed by Minnesota second baseman Chuck Knoblauch. Even with Smith at third and nobody out, the Braves failed to score and lost 1–0 in 10 innings.

0 Extra-inning World Series seventh games in 67 years. Between 1924 and 1991, no Game 7 went into extra innings. But then Jack Morris pitched Minnesota to a 1–0, 10-inning win over Atlanta in the final game of the 1991 World Series, which featured five extra-inning games.

0 Losses by Randy Johnson or Curt Schilling during 2001 World Series. The Arizona aces went 4–0 as the D'backs beat the Yankees in seven games. That followed a regular season when the pair combined for 665 strikeouts and Johnson averaged 13.4 strikeouts per nine innings, both records. Between them, they had 43 victories.

0 World championships won by the Cubs between 1908 and 2016—a 108-year stretch of futility unlikely to be matched.

0 Teammates before 2017 to lead off a 10th inning of a World Series game with consecutive homers. That's when Jose Altuve and Carlos Correa of the Astros did it in Game 2. Nine months later, two more Astros—Alex Bregman and George Springer—did it in the All-Star Game. In the regular season, however, no pair of Astros ever started the fateful 10th with home runs.

0 Elimination games Atlanta Braves played in 2021 postseason. While winning 11 of 17 postseason games en route to the world championship, the Braves never faced elimination.

0 Players who won World Series MVP awards with three different teams. Reggie Jackson did it twice (1973 A's and 1977 Yankees) and remains the only man to win it with multiple teams.

0 World Series MVPs from losing National League teams. The first winner from a losing American League team was Bobby Richardson of the 1960 Yankees, who lost to Pittsburgh when Bill Mazeroski led off a 9–9 game in the home ninth with a solo home run.

0 Pitchers to appear in all seven World Series games before 1973. Darold Knowles of the winning Oakland Athletics became the first reliever to do that.

0 World Series MVP awards for Bruce Hurst. The star pitcher for the Boston Red Sox was about to be named Most Valuable Player in the 1986 World Series when the Mets rallied for three runs with two outs in the home tenth inning of Game 6. Assuming the Series was ending, writers conducted their MVP balloting and the Shea Stadium scoreboard inadvertently flashed

a brief message that read CONGRATULATIONS, RED SOX. Both had to be changed when the Mets won Game 7—and the Series—two nights later.

0 American Leaguers who swept the competing World Series MVP awards. The SPORT Magazine World Series MVP award, first presented in 1955, became the Willie Mays World Series MVP award in 2017. The Babe Ruth Award, created by the New York chapter of the Baseball Writers Association of America, also honored a World Series MVP but was revised in 2003 to honor the best postseason performer in any given year. Before SPORT folded in 2000, no American Leaguers swept both. In fact, Sandy Koufax was the only player to sweep both awards twice (1963 and 1965), though fellow Dodger Johnny Podres was the first to win both for the same World Series (1955). Jack Morris also won two Babe Ruth awards, while Bob Gibson, Reggie Jackson, and Koufax won the SPORT award twice each. Different players won the competing World Series MVP awards for the first time in 1958 (Bob Turley and Elston Howard).

0 American Leaguers to be MVP for the season, Championship Series, and World Series. National Leaguer Willie Stargell was the only man to do that, in 1979, though he shared NL MVP honors with Keith Hernandez.

0 Games Bill Buckner finished at first base before his World Series error. The gimpy first baseman had been replaced by Dave Stapleton in every previous postseason game in the fall of 1986, but Boston manager John McNamara wanted him to be on the field when the Red Sox clinched. That never happened because the series was prolonged when Buckner let a Mookie Wilson grounder get between his legs as the winning run scored.

0 World championships for the Boston Red Sox between 1918 and 2004. The team came close in 1986 but failed to seal the deal despite 12 potential elimination pitches. Their opponent, the New York Mets, became the first team to win a World Series after being one strike away from elimination.

0 Traffic worries for the Boone brothers. Future major leaguers Aaron and Bret Boone dodged departing Dodger Stadium traffic after the opener of the 1988 World Series by sharing a scooter. They left immediately after Kirk Gibson's two-out, two-run, pinch-hit homer beat Oakland closer Dennis Eckersley for Los Angeles.

0 Teams that won 15 straight World Series games. The Yankees had 14 before the Mets ended the streak during the Subway Series of 2000.

0 All-Chicago World Series since 1906. Both the White Sox and Cubs had long droughts between championships, with the latter's lasting a record 108 years before it ended in 2016.

0 All-Los Angeles World Series. The Angels, a 1962 expansion team, have reached the Fall Classic only once, in 2002, after getting there as a wild-card team.

0 World Series with just Bay Area teams since 1989. The A's swept the Giants in the '89 World Series, which was interrupted 10 days after an earthquake. They have not met since.

0 Wild-card teams that won World Series before 1997. The Marlins were the first—and later did it again. In fact, Miami has won two world championships without ever winning a division title.

0 World Series MVP awards for Bryce Harper. When Bryce Harper signed a 13-year, $330 million contract with the Philadelphia Phillies on March 1, 2019, it contained a clause stipulating a $100,000 bonus if he won a World Series MVP award. In his first 10 seasons, however, Harper never even played for a pennant-winning team and had yet to reach the Fall Classic.

0 Players with 30 postseason homers. Manny Ramirez holds the record with 29 in 77 games.

All-Star Game

0 Managers ejected from All-Star games. Not even Bobby Cox, who had a record 158 ejections plus three more in postseason play.

0 Pitchers since 1935 to throw six innings in an All-Star Game. Lefty Grove's record seems safe.

0 All-Star Games played in 1945 because of wartime travel restrictions.

0 Black All-Stars before 1949. Jackie Robinson, Roy Campanella, Don Newcombe, and Larry Doby all played in that All-Star Game, two years after Robinson broke the color line.

0 All-Star Games won by the National League at an American League park before 1950. That summer, a 14th-inning Red Schoendienst homer in Comiskey Park gave the NL a 4–3 win—its first as a visitor in All-Star history, dating back to 1933. The first extra-inning All-Star Game, it was also the first shown on network television.

0 All-Star appearances for Preacher Roe in 1950 and 1951. The lefty spent the 1950 All-Star Game on the bench and also failed to get into the '51 game even though he was compiling one of the best winning percentages in baseball history.

0 At-bats for Pee Wee Reese in the 1951 All-Star Game. Selected for the fifth straight season in 1951, he spent most of that game on the bench behind Alvin Dark of the Giants. Reese went in for defense but did not bat.

0 All-Star winning pitchers other than Dean Stone who never threw a pitch. In the 1954 game at Municipal Stadium, Cleveland, Stone entered a tie game in the eighth and was on the mound when Red Schoendienst tried to steal home. He got the runner and was pitcher of record when the AL scored two in the ninth inning of an 11–9 victory.

0 American Leaguers to start two All-Star games in one year. National Leaguer Don Drysdale was the only pitcher to do that. It happened in 1962, the last of four years when the leagues played two All-Star games to raise revenue for the players' pension fund.

0 National Leaguers with All-Star grand slams. The only man to connect with the bases full was Fred Lynn in 1983, when the American League won the 50th anniversary All-Star Game at Comiskey Park with a resounding 13–3 win. The AL not only scored the most runs in All-Star history that day but twice tied their record, in 1992 and 1998.

0 Games played by Mike Schmidt six weeks before the 1989 All-Star Game. The fading Philadelphia slugger had announced

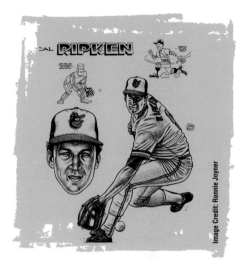

Image Credit: Ronnie Joyner

0 American Leaguers with 20 straight All-Star selections. After winning AL Rookie of the Year honors in 1982, Cal Ripken Jr. made the AL All-Star squad an AL-record 19 straight seasons (1983–2001). Hank Aaron holds the record with 21 straight years, one more than Willie Mays and Stan Musial, but all were National Leaguers.

his retirement May 29 but fans, recognizing his name, still elected him an All-Star starter. Schmidt showed up in uniform, but Howard Johnson of the New York Mets started at third base for the National League.

0 All-Stars injured during the team picture before 1996. That was the year Roberto Hernandez slipped, fell, and inadvertently punched Cal Ripken Jr. while trying to regain his balance. The Iron Man infielder suffered a broken nose, but it did not interfere with his consecutive games playing streak.

0 National Leaguers with 15 consecutive All-Star Game starts. Willie Mays had 14 in a row before American League icon Cal Ripken Jr. started his 15th straight in 1998.

0 All-Star pitchers who fanned the first four hitters before 1999. That was the year Pedro Martinez, a Red Sox pitcher backed by a friendly Fenway Park crowd, became the first to fan the first four men he faced.

0 Inside-the-park homers in All-Star play before 2007. There were 166 home runs in the All-Star Game, dating back to 1933, before Ichiro Suzuki hit the lone inside-the-park shot in San Francisco during the 2007 game. The ball struck a corner of the wall at AT&T Park and caromed away from Ken Griffey Jr.

0 American League wins in the first 10 extra-inning All-Star games. The AL finally won its first extra-inning All-Star Game, 4–3, in the 15-inning 2008 game at Yankee Stadium.

0 Home runs hit by Todd Frazier during 63 games preceding the 2015 All-Star Game in Cincinnati. After the longest home run drought of his career, he entered into the Home Run Derby anyway and actually won it.

0 Years before or after 2018 with 10 All-Star homers. When 10 different hitters connected, they set a record not only for All-Star Games but for all games. The game, played at Nationals Park in Washington, wound up as an 8–6, 10-inning victory for the American League.

0 Players who hit for the cycle in the All-Star Game. Since veteran stars don't always play the whole game, the odds are against it anyway.

0 All-Star Game MVPs before Maury Wills. The Dodgers shortstop won the award the first year it was given, for the 1962 game at D.C. Stadium in Washington.

0 All-Star MVPs not old enough to vote. The youngest All-Star Game MVP was Vlad Guerrero Jr. in 2021. His age was 22 years and 119 days.

0 Players with more than six All-Star homers. Stan Musial hit an even half-dozen for the record.

0 Years a dozen All-Stars were dealt at the trade deadline. The most to change uniforms were 10, in 2021, when those moved were Kris Bryant, Nelson Cruz, Eduardo Escobar, Adam Frazier, Joey Gallo, Kyle Gibson, Craig Kimbrel, Max Scherzer, Kyle Schwarber, and Trea Turner.

0 Players other than Mike Trout with consecutive All-Star MVPs.

Also Worth Noting

0 Pennant race tiebreakers before 1908. When the New York Giants and Chicago Cubs both finished at 98–55 that year, a playoff was needed. The Cubs won, 4–2, in that makeup of "the Fred Merkle" game. The Giants had lost a sure win over Chicago when the Merkle game was ruled a 1–1 tie that would have to be replayed if the teams finished in tie, which they did.

0 Teams that won more than 10 straight elimination games. The San Francisco Giants won exactly that many in 2010, 2012, and 2014, all world championship years.

0 Homers hit left-handed by Ozzie Smith in eight seasons. The switch-hitting St. Louis shortstop hit his first lefty homer in the last inning of a game that gave the Cards a 3–2 win over the Los Angeles Dodgers in Game 5 of the 1985 NL Championship Series. Another ninth-inning homer—by Jack Clark—gave the Cards the pennant two days later.

0 Hits by the Cincinnati Reds in the 2010 NL Division Series opener against Philadelphia. Roy Halladay's no-hitter came against the highest-scoring club in the National League that year.

0 Little League Classics before 2017.

0 Inside-the-corn home runs before Aaron Judge connected in the first Field of Dreams game. Played on a diamond surrounded by an Iowa cornfield, the Yankees-White Sox game featured eight home runs, including a massive jolt by Judge that disappeared into the corn.

0 Wins for Dodgers against Giants in pennant playoffs. Before the advent of divisional play in 1969, the Dodgers finished in flat-footed ties four times. They lost to St. Louis in 1946, lost to the Giants in 1951 and 1962, but beat the Milwaukee Braves in 1959. Both Dodgers losses to the Giants came in the ninth inning.

0 Confidence that leads are "safe." In 2011, the Boston Red Sox blew a nine-game lead with a 7–20 September mark that allowed the Tampa Bay Rays to win their last game and the American League wild card. That same season, the Atlanta Braves blew the NL wild card by dropping their final five and 18 of their last 26 after leading the Cards by 10 1/2 games on August 25 and 8 1/2 on September 1.

0 Wins for Atlanta Braves in four-homer games. Most teams win when one of their players hits four home runs in a game. But the Atlanta Braves lost when Bob Horner had a four-homer game against the Montreal Expos in 1986. The Boston Braves won in 1896 when Bobby Lowe hit four in a game (including two in an inning) and the Milwaukee Braves won when Joe Adcock hit four against the Brooklyn Dodgers in 1955. But the team lost when Braves pitchers yielded four homers to Hall of Famers Gil Hodges in 1950 and Willie Mays in 1961.

Etc.

0 Modern fielders wearing two gloves at once. Charles C. Waitt, with St. Louis of the National Association in 1875, wore gloves on both hands—even though most players of his era wore none. Jeered by other players, he set a precedent that others eventually followed. As the original tiny gloves grew in size, players started wearing them only on their non-throwing hand.

0 Games witnessed by Jack Norworth when he wrote *Take Me Out To the Ballgame*. He finally saw one 34 years later.

0 Black umpires in the early Negro Leagues. The leagues used white umps during their first two seasons.

0 Rules against rocking chairs in contracts. The New York Giants were tempted to add such prohibitions after pitching star Freddie Fitzsimmons crushed his fingers while sitting on a rocker and embroiled in conversation with Rogers Hornsby and Bill Terry. His absence cost the team the 1927 National League pennant, won by the Pittsburgh Pirates instead. Fat Freddie finished with 217 career victories while playing for the Giants and Dodgers.

0 Official games played by Robert Ripley. The "Believe It Or Not" founder had a 1913 New York Giants tryout as a pitcher but didn't pass. After becoming famous, the cartoonist-turned-collector got

0 Movies Rogers Hornsby saw during his playing days. The two-time Triple Crown winner, whose .358 lifetime average is a long-standing National League record, worried that watching films in the dark would ruin his eyes for batting.

Image Credit: Ronnie Joyner

into a 1939 exhibition game that included retired superstars Babe Ruth and Walter Johnson. Ripley's syndicated cartoons often contained baseball references.

0 Mentions of Eddie Sullivan in baseball records. It was the pseudonym used by Eddie Collins, who played for the Philadelphia Athletics while still captain of the Columbia University team.

0 Days Lou Gehrig spent in the minors. He went directly from Columbia College to the majors.

0 Limits to suspensions resulting from Black Sox Scandal. Beyond the original Eight Men Out, all members of the notorious 1919 Chicago White Sox banned for involvement in an alleged World Series fix, dozens of other players were banned or suspended, usually for reasons involving gambling, lack of integrity, or consorting with undesirable elements.

0 Truth to the theory that the grand jury in the 1920 Black Sox trial was unaware of the damaging testimony from players. Although the confessions were stolen, the testimony they contained were recreated by stenographers and read back to the jury that eventually acquitted them.

0 Financial losses for Black Sox players. After word of the game-fixing scandal broke in 1920, White Sox owner Charley Comiskey released the seven accused players and gave everyone else bonus checks that represented the difference between winners' shares and losers' shares from the World Series pot.

0 Postwar field announcers. After the New York Giants installed baseball's first public address system in 1929, the need for field announcers with big voices and oversized megaphones gradually evaporated. Jack Lenz, who worked at the Polo Grounds and Yankee Stadium, shouted lineups, batteries, and subs for some 2,000 consecutive games.

0 Moe Berg games seen by his father. One of the smartest men in major-league history, Berg was a good-fielding but light-hitting catcher whose lifetime batting average was .243. But he spoke more than a dozen languages and secretly worked for the OSS, forerunner of the CIA, during World War II. His father boycotted his games because he thought Moe was wasting his considerable intellect.

0 Batting practice pitchers before 1937. Paul Schreiber, who once pitched for the Brooklyn Dodgers, was the first man hired for that job, by the 1937 Yankees.

Image Credit: Ronnie Joyner

0 Triple Crowns for Babe Ruth (above) and Joe DiMaggio (below). Though both were sluggers who also hit for average, the Yankees stars never led the American League in hitting, homers, and runs batted in at the same time—a feat Ted Williams of the Red Sox did twice.

0 Helmets worn by Mickey Cochrane. The player-manager of the 1937 Detroit Tigers suffered a fractured skull when hit by a pitch, lay unconscious for 10 days, and never played again.

0 Ballpark organists before the war. The Chicago Cubs broke through by installing an organ at Wrigley Field in 1941.

0 Wins by Japanese All-Stars against visiting American team led by Babe Ruth. Fans didn't seem to mind. They cheered Ruth, who hit 13 home runs during the 16-game exhibition series swept by the US team after the 1934 season.

0 Games Pie Traynor drove to. The Hall of Fame third baseman never learned to drive a car.

0 Baseball broadcasts before 1920. That was the year KDKA in Pittsburgh aired the first game.

0 Night games before 1935. The Cincinnati Reds then played a night game at Crosley Field on May 24 against Philadelphia, winning 2–1.

0 Catching experience by Josh Gibson when he volunteered to catch. A team needed a catcher and Gibson, sitting in the stands, grabbed the opportunity. He went on to become the Babe Ruth of the Negro Leagues.

0 Old-Timers' games before 1947. That's when the Yankees held the first of many. Prior to that, teams sometimes suited up former stars for token appearances long after they retired.

0 Jimmie Foxx moonshots. Although he hit 534 home runs, trailing only Babe Ruth's 714 at the time of his retirement, Double X never actually hit one to the moon. But he hit many of them a long way. As Hall of Fame pitcher Lefty Gomez explained, "When Neil Armstrong first set foot on the moon in 1969, he and all the space scientists were puzzled by an unidentifiable white object. I knew immediately what it was: a home run ball hit off me in 1933 by Jimmie Foxx!"

Image Credit: Ronnie Joyner

Image Credit: Ronnie Joyner

0 Players who enlisted before Bob Feller. The first major leaguer to sign up for World War II military service after Pearl Harbor, Feller won eight battle stars during a four-year stint as tail-gunner on the USS *Alabama*. That wartime service precluded his membership in The 300-win club (he finished with 266 victories).

0 Men who played for the Dodgers, Knicks, and Rangers. Organist Gladys Goodding, a woman, made her Ebbets Field debut in 1942 and later worked for New York's basketball and hockey teams.

0 Ebbets Field games attended by Vin Scully before he broadcast one. Before he became the longtime Voice of the Dodgers in both Brooklyn and Los Angeles, Scully was a New York Giants fan who grew up in the Bronx, where he was born in the middle of Yankees territory.

0 Decent views of 1948 Cleveland World Series game for fans in roped-off sections. When 86,288 fans showed up for Game 5 at Municipal Stadium, which had a capacity of 78,000, more than

Image Credit: Ronnie Joyner

0 Four-letter athletes at UCLA before Jackie Robinson. En route to desegregating Major League Baseball with the 1947 Brooklyn Dodgers, Robinson lettered in baseball, basketball, football, and track at UCLA. He then won a batting title, Rookie of the Year trophy, and MVP award in the National League, winding up in the Baseball Hall of Fame.

6,000 paid $5 each to stand in a roped-off section of the outfield—even though they couldn't see through the thick crowd.

0 Widely televised games before the Second World War. With only a handful of TV sets in use, the Brooklyn Dodgers broadcast a doubleheader from Ebbets Field on August 26, 1939. The pioneer station was W2XBS and Red Barber was the announcer. It would be nine more years before the first regional telecast, a Cubs-White Sox exhibition game originating from Chicago's WGN with Jack Brickhouse behind the mic.

0 Color telecasts of baseball before 1951. That year, fans were not only buzzing about Brooklyn's big lead on August 11 but also that day's NBC telecast of a Braves-Dodgers doubleheader. Few had televisions and almost none had access to the brand-new color technology but knew change was in the offing.

0 At-bats for Donald Davidson, a four-foot-tall Boston Braves batboy who later became traveling secretary for the team in all three of its host cities. Sent up to bat for Moe Berg in an actual game, he was sent back to the dugout by the home-plate umpire. But Bill Veeck must have been watching since he hired a midget, formally put him on the roster, and actually got him an official at-bat for the St. Louis Browns in 1951.

0 Female major leaguers. Eleanor Engle, though signed to play shortstop for the Harrisburg Senators in 1952, came closest but never got her chance when the signing news created a furor. She worked out before the June 22 game but never played.

Image Credit: Ronnie Joyner

0 Players who out-homered Harmon Killebrew during the '60s. The slugging corner infielder of the Minnesota Twins hit 393 of his 573 career homers during the decade, leading the American League five times.

0 At-bats for sprinter Herb Washington, who stole 25 bases for the 1974 Oakland A's while used exclusively as a pinch-runner.

0 Appreciation of Yankees by the actress who played Eleanor Gehrig. Theresa Wright, Lou Gehrig's wife in the 1941 film *Pride of the Yankees*, didn't appreciate the history of the team until the '90s.

0 Interleague games before 1997. In an effort to boost attendance in the wake of the 232-day player strike that wiped out parts of the 1994 and 1995 seasons, Major League Baseball added interleague games to its schedule in 1997. Most of the games were regional, such as Yankees-Mets or Cubs-White Sox, but the concept created controversy over the sanctity of long-standing league records. To smooth the transition, MLB merged the separate umpiring staffs three years later.

0 Invitations to Yankees Old-Timers' Day for Jim Bouton. After writing *Ball Four*, the first tell-all baseball book, Bouton was banned from Yankee Stadium by team owner George Steinbrenner. The 28-year exile ended after publication of an open letter from the former pitcher's son. Bouton got a standing ovation when he came to Old-Timers' Day in 1998.

0 Fine imposed on Mike Piazza after Roger Clemens beaning. Although beanball incidents usually produce punishment for both sides, that was not the case with Roger Clemens vs. Mike Piazza. On July 8, 2000, the Mets catcher suffered a concussion when hit on the head by a Clemens pitch in the first inning and had to miss the All-Star Game. When they met again in World Series Game 2, Clemens broke his bat on a foul ball. Clemens grabbed it and appeared to throw it at him as Piazza ran toward first. The Yankees pitcher was slapped with a $50,000 fine.

0 Cheers for Steve Bartman in Chicago. An avid Cubs fan, he prevented the team from winning the 2003 National League pennant by interfering with a foul ball left fielder Moises Alou was ready to catch. Five outs away, the Cubs collapsed, allowing the Marlins to score eight runs in the eighth inning of Game 6 and win the last two games of the NL Championship Series. Bitter Cubs fans hounded Bartman, who was eventually given a ring by the team after the Cubs won the 2016 World Series—ending a championship drought that had lasted 108 years.

0 Missed broadcasts for John Sterling. He broadcast 5,060 consecutive Yankees games, calling every Derek Jeter at-bat, every Mariano Rivera pitch, and the last outs of five world championship seasons, before reducing his road game schedule at age 84 in 2022.

0 Players whose parents won Academy Awards. The closest was longtime executive Theo Epstein, grandson of Philip G. Epstein, Oscar winner for writing the classic film *Casablanca*. Theo Epstein's teams have included two world champions, the Boston Red Sox and Chicago Cubs.

0 Players who missed the Hall of Fame by one vote. With 75 percent required for election in the "regular" voting by the Baseball Writers Association of America, no one ever missed by a single vote. Three missed by two, however: Craig Biggio in 2014, Nellie Fox in 1984, and Pie Traynor in 1947.

0 Women elected to Cooperstown in the twentieth century. The first was Effa Manley, the late owner of the Newark Eagles, a Negro Leagues team. When elected in 2006, she became the first female member of the Baseball Hall of Fame.

0 Female big leaguers. Some tried, however. Jackie Mitchell, a 17-year-old lefty, fanned Babe Ruth and Lou Gehrig in an exhibition game and multi-sport star Babe Didrikson Zaharias pitched for big-league teams in spring training before joining the barnstorming House of David.

0 Women who managed in the All-American Girls Professional Baseball League. All the teams had male managers until the Kalamazoo Lassies hired Bonnie Baker to finish the 1950 season.

0 Hall of Famers after Al Kaline to sign in their prom suits. Signed at 16, he came downstairs to sign, then made his debut for Detroit in 1953 and was employed by the Tigers for six decades.

0 Flights for American League MVP. Boston Red Sox outfielder Jackie Jensen, the 1958 American League MVP, hated flying so much he once drove 800 miles from Boston to Detroit rather than join the team plane. He actually quit the game at 32, sitting out the 1960 season, before returning with the help of hypnotists and psychiatrists. After an off-year in 1961, he quit for good.

0 National anthems sung by Jim Thome. The Hall of Famer's daughter Lisa, representing the family, sang it in Cooperstown after practicing at the podium in front of an empty field.

0 Hall of Fame files on actor Martin Sheen. But there is a file on his son Charlie Sheen, star of *Major League*, in the institution's library.

0 Peace treaty pictures after labor dispute. Negotiations between owners and players were so bitter in 1981 that union chief Marvin Miller and owners rep Ray Grebey refused to pose together for the traditional "peace treaty" picture.

0 Princess Poc-a-Homa sightings. Signed by the Braves as the distaff half of Braves mascot Chief Noc-a-Homa in the '80s, she was fired when Levi Walker—the male mascot—claimed his contract entitled him to be the club's lone mascot.

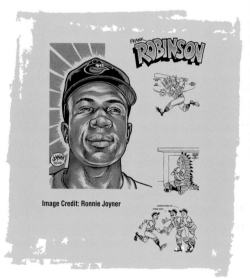

Image Credit: Ronnie Joyner

0 Players with MVP awards in both leagues – except for Frank Robinson. He won with the 1961 Reds and 1966 Orioles, capturing the first American League Triple Crown since Mickey Mantle in 1956. He then became the first black manager, with the Cleveland Indians, in 1975.

Image Credit: Ronnie Joyner

0 Reasons to lift Fergie Jenkins for a pinch-hitter. In 1971, more than 50 years before the designated hitter came to the National League, the lanky right-hander of the Chicago Cubs hit .243 with six homers and 20 runs batted in.

0 Twins for Twins until 2000. The Minnesota Twins, named for the Twin Cities of Minneapolis and St. Paul, had no players who fathered twins until Denny Hocking, a career .251 hitter who obviously did better in the fatherhood department.

0 Twentieth-century big-leaguers in the college football and college basketball Halls of Fame. Dick Groat, who also spent a year in the NBA, became the first in 2011. A shortstop who won two World Series rings during his 14-year career, the longtime Pirate also led the NL in turning double plays five times—a major-league mark.

0 Confidence in his own ability shown by Jackie Bradley Jr. He once doubted his skills so much that he kept his home in

KING HENRY AARON

Image Credit: Ronnie Joyner

0 Times Hank Aaron hit for the cycle. The first Atlanta Brave to collect a single, double, triple, and home run in the same game was the otherwise-forgettable Albert Hall. Aaron never did it.

Robert **REDFORD**

Image Credit: Ronnie Joyner

0 Years Robert Redford played high school baseball with Don Drysdale. While they did attend Van Nuys High School together and the future star of *The Natural* was on the tennis team, they were not teammates on the school's baseball team. Redford did play some college ball at the University of Colorado, however, before leaving for New York to pursue his acting dreams.

Pawtucket, top farm club of the Red Sox, and commuted 50 miles each way to Boston.

0 Names listed on Baseball Hall of Fame ballots by six different voters in 2022. They left their ballots blank as a protest against all players eligible for election, as well as the continued exclusion of the suspended Pete Rose.

0 Six-decade players. Three players whose careers spanned *five* decades: Nick Altrock, Minnie Minoso, and Julio Franco.

Baseball Hall of Fame, *So You Think You Know Baseball*, Coral Gables, FL: Mango Publishing, 2021.

Benagh, Jim, *Baseball: Startling Stories Behind the Records*, New York: Sterling Publishing, 1987.

Berger, Dave, *Take Me Out to the Ball Game: Comical and Freakish Injuries We Cannot Make Up*, Georgetown, TX: Baseball Injury Publishers, 2020.

The Bill James Handbook 2022: The Complete, Up-to-Date Statistics on Every Major-League Player, Team, and Manager Through Last Season, Chicago: ACTA Publications, 2021.

Binkley, Jim and Eisenhammer, Fred, *Baseball's Most Memorable Trades*, Jefferson, NC, McFarland, 1997.

Blake, Mike, *The Incomplete Book of Baseball Superstitions, Rituals, and Oddities*, New York: Wynwood Press, 1991.

Blomberg, Ron, and Dan Schlossberg, *Designated Hebrew: The Ron Blomberg Story*, New York: Sports Publishing, 2006.

Bloom, Howard, and Michael Kun, *The Baseball Uncyclopedia: a Highly-Opinionated, Myth-Busting Guide to the Great American Game*, Cincinnati: Emmis Books, 2006.

Bock, Hal, *Banned: Baseball's Blacklist of All-Stars and Also-Rans*, New York: Diversion Books, 2017.

Chuck, Bill, and Jim Kaplan, *Walkoffs, Last Licks, and Final Outs: Baseball's Grand (and Not-So-Grand) Finales*, Skokie, IL: ACTA Sports, 2008.

Clark, Al with Dan Schlossberg, *Called Out But Safe: a Baseball Umpire's Journey*, Lincoln, NE: University of Nebraska Press, 2014.

Fingers, Rollie, and Yellowstone Ritter, *Rollie's Follies: A Hall of Fame Revue of Baseball Stories and Stats, Lists, and Lore*, Cincinnati: Clerisy Press, 2009.

Finley, Nancy, *Finley Ball, How Two Outsiders Turned the Oakland A's Into a Dynasty and Changed the Game Forever*, Washington, DC: Regnery History, 2016.

Frommer, Harvey, *Baseball's Greatest Records, Streaks, and Feats*, New York: Atheneum, 1983.

Hamilton, Milo, and Dan Schlossberg with Bob Ibach, *Making Airwaves: 60 Years at Milo's Microphone*, New York: Sports Publishing, 2007.

Hoppel, Joe and Craig Carter, *The Sporting News Baseball Trivia Book*, St. Louis: *The Sporting News*, 1983.

———, *The Sporting News Baseball Trivia 2*, St. Louis: *The Sporting News*, 1987.

Johnstone, Jay, with Rick Talley, *Over the Edge: Baseball's Uncensored Exploits From WAY Out in Left Field*, Chicago: Contemporary Books, 1987.

_____, *Some of My Best Friends Are Crazy: Baseball's Favorite Lunatic Goes In Search of His Peers*, New York: Macmillan, 1990.

_____, *Temporary Insanity*, Chicago: Contemporary Books, 1985.

Kurkjian, Tim, *Is This a Great Game or What?: From A-Rod's Heart to Zim's Head—My 25 Years in Baseball*, New York: St. Martin's Press, 2007.

Light, Jonathan Fraser, *The Cultural Encyclopedia of Baseball, 2nd edition*, Jefferson, NC: McFarland, 2005.

Lucas, Ed and Christopher Lucas, *Seeing Home: the Ed Lucas Story: a Blind Broadcaster's Story of Overcoming Life's Greatest Obstacles*, New York: Simon & Schuster, 2015.

Lyons, Douglas B., *The Baseball Geek's Bible: All the Facts and Stats You'll Ever Need*, London: MQ Publications Ltd., 2006.

Lyons, Douglas B. and Jeffrey Lyons, *Curveballs and Screwballs: Over 1,286 Incredible Baseball Facts, Finds, Flukes, and More*, New York: Random House, 2001.

_____, *Out of Left Field: Over 1,134 Newly-Discovered Amazing Baseball Records, Connections, Coincidences, and More*, New York: Random House, 1998.

————, *Short Hops & Foul Tips: 1,734 Wild and Wacky Baseball Facts*, Lanham, MD: Taylor Trade, 2005.

McConnell, John, *Cooperstown by the Numbers: an Analysis of Baseball Hall of Fame Elections*, Jefferson, NC: McFarland, 2010.

Nadel, Eric, and Craig R. Wright, *The Man Who Stole First Base: Tales From Baseball's Past*, foreword by Bill James, Dallas, TX: Taylor Publishing, 1989.

————, *The Baseball Hall of Shame: the Most Outrageous Moments of All Time*, Guilford, CT: Lyons Press, 2012.

Nash, Bruce and Allan Zullo, *The Baseball Hall of Shame's Warped Record Book*, New York: Macmillan Publishing, 1991.

————, *Believe It Or Else (Baseball Edition)*, New York: Dell Publishing, 1992.

The National Baseball Hall of Fame Almanac, 2022 edition, Lynn, MA.: H.O. Zimman, Inc., 2022.

Nemec, David, *Incredible Baseball Trivia: More than 200 Hardball Questions for the Thinking Fan*, New York: Sports Publishing, 2019.

Schlossberg, Dan, *The Baseball IQ Challenge*, Chicago: Contemporary Books, 1998.

————, *BaseballLaffs*, Middle Village, NY: Jonathan David Publishers, 1982.

_____, *The New Baseball Bible: Notes, Nuggets, Lists, and Legends From Our National Pastime*, New York: Sports Publishing, 2020.

_____, *When the Braves Ruled the Diamond: Fourteen Flags Over Atlanta*, 2021 World Championship Edition, New York: Sports Publishing, 2022.

_____, *The Wit and Wisdom of Baseball: Single Quotes and Double Talk*, Lincolnwood, IL: Publications International, 1997.

Schnakenberg, Robert, *The Underground Baseball Encyclopedia: Baseball Stuff You Never Needed to Know and Can Certainly Live Without*, Chicago: Triumph Books, 2010.

Shlain, Bruce, *Oddballs: Baseball's Greatest Pranksters, Flakes, Hot Dogs, and Hotheads*, New York: Penguin, 1989.

Toropov, Brandon, *50 Biggest Baseball Myths*, Secaucus, NJ: Citadel Press, 1997.

Vanderberg, Bob, *Frantic Frank Lane: Baseball's Ultimate Wheeler-Dealer*, Jefferson, NC: McFarland, 2013.